Fayetteville Arkansas in the Civil War

by
Russell Mahan

2nd Edition 2019
Published by Historical Enterprises
HistoricalEnterprises@Outlook.com

Published by Historical Enterprises, Santa Clara, Utah
Copyright © 2003, 2019 by Russell L. Mahan

No part of this book may be reproduced, scanned, or distributed in any printed or electronic form without permission.

First Edition 2003
Second Edition January 2019
Printed in the United States of America
ISBN 9780999396247

Fayetteville Arkansas in the Civil War

Table of Contents

1860 Fayetteville on the Eve of War.
"A charming town set among the hills".................... 1

1861 Confederate Days.
"We have established ourselves free and
independent"... 37

1862 Destruction and Death.
"Fayetteville presented a sad spectacle...of
destruction and waste and ruin"......................... 59

1863 The Battle of Fayetteville.
"This splendid body of cavalry came thundering
down Dickson Street".................................... 87

1864 An Occupied Town in an Endless War.
"The business of killing men still goes bravely on."..... 117

1865 Peace from the East.
"All is now peace and tranquility here... I could
not have believed that such a change could have
taken place so soon.".................................. 131

Endnotes. 137

Index. 145

1860 Fayetteville on the Eve of War

"A charming town set down among the hills"

In Fayetteville, Arkansas, in 1860 the sounds of nature, of animals, birds and people, predominated then. There were no cars or trucks, no trains or planes, no steamships. Movement was as it had been from the beginning of time, at the speed of a person walking or riding a horse. There were no paved streets. Homes and businesses contained no electrical devices of any kind. People moved slowly in a quiet world. Of course, this is a view looking backward from nearly a century and a half. In the perspective of the people at the time, the world was fully modern, the most convenient ever.

Marian Tebbetts was born in Fayetteville in 1850 and lived there until 1862. Washington County Historical Society.

"Fayetteville was a charming town, set down among the hills and slopes of the Ozarks," said Marian Tebbetts, who as a girl of ten lived in Fayetteville in 1860. "Isolated from the outside world, a hundred miles from the railroad, fifty miles across the hills to the Arkansas River.... It was a little town, sufficient unto itself, depending on no one for religious, scholastic or social environment. Several churches, the Arkansas College, two good schools for girls and an active Masonic Lodge gave it strength and stability and the ability to furnish its own social entertainments."[1]

Fayetteville was a young town. It was young in its existence, having existed for just thirty-two years. Some of the original pioneers were still there. It always had been and still was isolated, lying on the periphery of the American nation and just twenty five miles from the Indian territories of modern Oklahoma. It was far from any significant population center, and not reachable by any navigable river, railroad, or well constructed highway. It was young in the makeup of its population, with a median age of just twenty-one years.

And yet already "Fayetteville was a center of religious and education influence, widely known as such over the state," wrote Robert Graham, one of the ministers in town. It "had two female colleges.... These added to the business, culture and education of the town. Families sought Fayetteville as a home while educating their children. A newspaper, *The Democrat*, was founded in 1860. A new courthouse was built, stores and residences increased. The whole town took on new life so that within a few years it was the handsomest little city in the state and so allowed by visitors and others."[2]

A new era opened up in the late 1850s when regular stagecoach service was brought to Fayetteville. This brought in travelers and news from the outside world as never before. In 1857 Congress established a mail route from St. Louis to San Francisco, taking a route southward through Springfield, Missouri, to Fayetteville, Arkansas, and on to Fort Smith, then turning westward into the Indian Territory. The contract was for six years at $600,000 per year, requiring that the mail and up to nine passengers be carried at least twice per week. The route was 2,800 miles in length, and the stage fare was $200 for the twenty-two-day trip that included 140 stops at way stations. There had been prior stage lines into Fayetteville owned by two town doctors, Thomas Pollard and Wade Pollard, but they sold out their much more limited service to this ambitious new project.

The contract was awarded to John Butterfield of New York, who established the Overland Mail Company. He rode the route himself, and was so favorably impressed with Fayetteville that he sent his own son, Charles, to manage the stop there. The station was established on the west side of College Avenue at Center Street, and a 360-acre ranch west of town was also purchased. Service began on September 15, 1858, with a stage rolling southwest bound out of St. Louis. "Remember boys," Butterfield told his stage drivers, "nothing on God's earth must stop the mail!"[3]

John Butterfield himself rode the first stage. His passenger was Waterman L. Ormsby, a 23-year-old journalist for *The New York*

Herald, who was going the entire route to San Francisco. Ormsby wrote a series of articles detailing his adventure. Going on a poor road over steep and rugged hills, it took three hours to go the final twelve miles to Fayetteville.

A sketch of Fayetteville from "Battles and Leaders of the Civil War," looking from East Mountain toward the west.

"This town," he wrote after arriving, "is located up among the hills, in the most inaccessible spot in [the] county, said by its inhabitants to be the star county of the state. It has two churches, the county court house, a number of fine stores and dwellings, and, I believe, about 1,800 inhabitants. It is a flourishing little town; and its deficiency of a good hotel will, I understand, be supplied by Mr. Butterfield, who has bought some property for that purpose. He is the most energetic president of a company I ever saw. He appears to know every foot of the ground and to be known by everybody...."[4]

Ormsby's comment about the deficiency of a good local hotel would not have found favor with the Taylor family. Margaret Taylor, 22, was the granddaughter of James Byrnside, the founder of what became Byrnside's Hotel. In 1860 it was not a modern hotel such as Ormsby would have known in New York City, but rather was an old fashioned tavern. It was operated by Margaret and her husband, 27-year-old Isaac Taylor, with the considerable assistance of thirty-five slaves.

The town of Fayetteville was laid out in a full, square section of land,* with streets running at right angles. However, the blocks were not all the same size, and although the streets were straight they were far from level because the town was larger than the hill it topped. Byrnside's Hotel was located at the heart of the town on a corner of the town square. At the center of the square was the county courthouse, built in 1855. Other hotels in town were operated by John Onstott (the oldest man in town at the age of 71) and James Darneal.

"When the stage horn sounded at the Gunter place [on the northeast corner of town]...the Byrnsides would put the meal on the table, and the stable boys would have six fresh horses harnessed ready for the relay.... The coming of the stage was the day's event... Mail was carried by stage, as was luggage. It brought many students to Arkansas College."[5]

Instant long distance communications came to Fayetteville on July 4, 1860. The Stebbins Telegraph Company sent a gang of linemen down from Springfield, Missouri, approximately along the same route as the Overland Stage, after which it became known both as "Telegraph Road" and "the Wire Road." The line was strung on trees where possible, and on poles where necessary. On this eighty-fourth anniversary of the Declaration of Independence Fayetteville attorney James R. Pettigrew sent a telegram to the mayor of St. Louis, who responded in kind.[6] Tracy Simon, a 37-year-old single man born in Connecticut, was the resident telegraph operator in town in 1860. The world was getting closer to Fayetteville, and within just one more year, it would get very much closer.

Fayetteville was chartered as a city by the State of Arkansas in 1859. In the elections held at that time, J.W. Walker was selected as Mayor. The City Council consisted of attorney Elias D. Boudinot, Charles E. Butterfield of the stage line, Addison Crouch, J.B. Simpson, and merchant James H. Stirman. Peter Van Hoose was the school commissioner.

In the middle of July 1860 U.S. Assistant Marshal J.H. Parks arrived in town. He went door to door throughout Fayetteville, speaking with every family and compiling information. The work he did was part of the major effort to fulfill the command of the United States Constitution that a census of the people be taken every ten

---

* Section 16, Township 16 North. Range 30 West of the Fifth Principal Meridian in Washington County, Arkansas.

years. His work between July 13th and 17th ultimately reported that within the city limits of Fayetteville resided 967 people.* Of that number, 671 were whites (70% of the total), 294 were slaves (30%), and two were Indians.⁷ It is fair to say that upwards of another eight hundred to a thousand souls lived in the nearby vicinity but beyond the city limits, and that about two thousand people would have likely said they lived in Fayetteville.**

Parks was a veteran census taker by then, for the first house he visited on July 13th in Fayetteville was numbered as the 946th dwelling he had approached. By chance this first home was occupied by Joseph Zellieh and his wife Charlotta. He was 29 years old, born in "Hungaria." Unfamiliar with the ethnic name, Parks wrote down "Cellik." Of the 671 whites in town, twenty-five, or 4% of the total population and 7% of the adult population, were born outside of the United States. Charlotta was 25, born in New York. She was one of sixty-five adults born in non-slaveholding states, or 20% of the total. By place of birth, then, the adult white make-up of Fayetteville was 73% Southern, 20% Northern and 7% foreign.

The Zelliehs, like many others enumerated that summer, did not belong to one of the prominent families of the area. Joseph was a barber, and owned personal property totaling just $25 in value. It is known that they rented their home because the census records that they owned no real estate. Living with them was John Cate, a twenty-three year old grocer born in Tennessee. The census reveals that it was very common in Fayetteville for more than one family to live in a single home. In the instructions given to Marshal Parks and all census takers, "by a dwelling house is meant a separate inhabited tenement, containing one or more families under one roof. Where several tenements are in one block, with walls...to divide them, having separate entrances, they are each to be numbered as separate houses,

---

* *Throughout history census takers have always missed a significant number of people in their enumeration. However, those counted and the information obtained from them provide a considerable basis for understanding Fayetteville just before the Civil War.*

** *Pastor William Baxter, President of the Arkansas College and a resident of town in 1860, stated that the population of Fayetteville at the beginning of the war was 2,000. Chaplain Francis Springer of the 10th Illinois Cavalry, who spent several weeks in town in 1862-1863, stated that the pre-war population was 1,800. Waterman L. Ormsby used the same number.*

but where not so divided, they are to be numbered as one house."[8]

The second house visited by J.H. Parks that summer day was that of William McGarrah. Here the marshal hit bedrock Fayetteville history and genealogy. McGarrah was one of the original settlers of the area, having come when the area was opened by a treaty with the Cherokees in 1828. He had owned much of the land on the northeast corner of town, and had opened the first store in the area. He was 61 years old, South Carolina-born, and a farmer. He valued his real estate at $15,000, a considerable sum in those days. However, the numbers furnished to the census takers must be warily considered, as some people feared they would be taxed on the value given. He stated his personal property to be worth $600. Even then, this was not much pf an accumulation for a lifetime.

Elizabeth McGarrah, the daughter of William and Elizabeth McGarrah. She was 17 years old in 1860. Shiloh Museum.

McGarrah's wife, Elizabeth, was 47 years old and born in Missouri. All of the four children remaining in the home, ranging in ages from 12 to 21, were born in Arkansas. This was a typical Fayetteville family; parents were born in other older Southern states and migrated to Arkansas where their children were born. Of the white population, half was twenty-one years or older, and half was younger. McGarrah owned five slaves, who ranged in age from five to twenty-five, and lived in a slave house on the property.

"The McGarrahs were of the true backwoods type," records Goodspeed's 1889 history of Washington County. "They were entirely uneducated, not able even to read or write." William had for a longtime been a grocer in Fayetteville, but because of his illiteracy he never kept any books. His brother, John, was twice elected to the Arkansas Legislature, where he diligently worked to conceal his illiteracy.[9]

Only nineteen adults in town could neither read nor write, and the McGarrahs were the only family where both the husband and the wife were in that category. This represents a white literacy rate of 94%, which is remarkable for the frontier, and certainly refutes the image, as far as Fayetteville is concerned, of an illiterate backward pioneer Arkansas. Yet the literacy of the people is no surprise. Fayetteville was then, as it is now, the leading educational center for Arkansas. The two younger McGarrah children, 16-year-old James and 12-year-old Sarah, attended school within the last year, as did most of the children in town.

In 1839 a woman by the name of Sophia Sawyer arrived in town and opened the Fayetteville Female Seminary. She was a compassionate, caring woman who found a cause as a missionary among the Cherokee people. She went west with them into the territory now known as Oklahoma. Now Miss Sawyer was fleeing from the Indian Nations in the wake of the murder of Chief John Ridge, who had signed the treaty agreeing that the tribe would remove to Oklahoma. With Sawyer was the chief's widow, Sara Ridge, and about fourteen Cherokee girls. They formed the starting class of the seminary.

By 1842 the school had grown to fifty students, and by the 1850s it had over one hundred. David and Jane Walker deeded some land on West Mountain Street, near town square, for the school. In 1850 the census showed thirteen of the

Sophia Sawyer, left, and her Fayetteville Female Seminary, as drawn by fellow townsman William Quesenbery. Washington County Historical Society.

young women living with Miss Sawyer, but that census was taken in October. The 1860 census, being taken in July, showed no students because school was out for the summer. Many of the local women of 1860 had attended there in their youth. Margaret Taylor, owner of Byrnside's Hotel, had attended for three years.

Newspaperman James M. Van Hoose later wrote that in 1852 "[m]any beautiful young ladies from Missouri, the Indian country, and South Arkansas attend this school." Sophia Sawyer died in 1854. Her students erected a memorial to her, a marble monument over a solitary grave at the rear of the building. "Sophia Sawyer, Died Feb 22, 1854, Aged 61 years. She Hath done what she could. Erected by her pupils."

The "first school house in the place was a log cabin, her next a room in the court house, & then the seminary which she reared with the proceeds of her scholastic labors. This edifice has undergone considerable changes since the decease of its founder. Though neither magnificent in dimension nor elegant in style, it is of ample capacity for a large school, & convenient in its arrangements, for the use to which it is devoted. A large boarding house on the same lot (about an acre) has been added since the demise of Miss Sawyer.[10]

Lucretia Foster succeeded the founder, and was still in charge of Seminary in 1860. By then she had married Jackson Smith, who soon died, but four years later she still wore black. The census recorded the Seminary teachers as Mary Daniels, 28 years old, Mary Clark, 23, Sallie Davidson, 18, Jane Feemster, 22-year-old music teacher, and her sister, 20-year-old Annie Feemster.

It was not the only educational institution in town. Educator Robert W. Mecklin in 1845 opened Ozark Institute about three miles to the northwest. There he operated a school for young men for about twelve years, teaching approximately one hundred students per year. The school closed in 1857.

Arkansas College was chartered in 1852, having been founded two years previously by Reverend Robert Graham, an English-born minister. He had come to Fayetteville in 1848 on an evangelical tour, and the people liked him. One of Fayetteville's merchants, J. Harvey Stirman, went all the way back to Pennsylvania on behalf of several townspeople to ask him to come back to be a resident minister of the

Reverend Robert Graham, below left, was the founder of Arkansas College. Reverend William Baxter, right, was the president of the College beginning in 1858. Author's Collection.

Christian Church. Graham agreed to do so. He was designated in the 1860 census as a "Campbellite preacher."*

As a means of supplementing the meager salary of a minister he taught school with Robert W. Mecklin. In 1850 Graham split off and formed his own school, Arkansas College, taking twenty Ozark students with him. One cannot help but feel that Mecklin was not very happy about this.

The new Arkansas College had a building constructed in 1852, with a library and two wings added later on a ten acre campus on the northeast corner of town on land formerly owned by the illiterate William McGarrah. Arkansas College drew local students as well as young men from nearby states and the Indian Nations. This school ave rise to the name of the north-south street that ran before it, thereafter called College Avenue. After several years Pastor Graham decided to leave Arkansas College, and brought in Pastor William Baxter, another English-born "Campbellite preacher," to lead the school. William Law

---

* The Campbellites were followers of Alexander Campbell, who from 1830 to 1866 was a nationally known religious theologian and prolific writer. His followers became known as the Disciples of Christ, or simply the Christian Church. It was a significant religious movement that still exists today.

was a 25-year-old mathematics professor at Arkansas College.

William Baxter left us the most detailed account of the Civil War in Fayetteville that we have. He was born in England in 1820, but came to the United States with his parents at the age of eight. After obtaining his religious credentials at Bethany College, he spent most of his time in the South. Nevertheless, he was a firm and unwavering unionist. A fellow minister in 1868 described him as "rather small of stature, but compactly built; has strongly-marked features, with a nervous, excitable temperament." He was also said to have a "warm, impulsive, and generous nature."[11] He was fond of writing, having published a book of poems in 1852 and regularly contributed to religious journals.

The Fayetteville Female Institute was founded in 1858 by Thomas B. Van Horne. It was housed in a two-story frame building with a tall spire. Teachers included Cornelia Corwin, a 21 year-old music teacher, Mary Howland, a 31-year-old sewing teacher, and Ferdinand Zellner, a 28-year-old music teacher who Marian Tebbetts Banes described as "a fine young Austrian, so highly educated in music as to have come to this country as one of Jenny Lind's first violinists." He had written a tune called "the Fayetteville Polka." Jonas M. Tebbetts was a supporter of the new school, and his daughter, Marian, who lived across the street to the east, attended. She called Miss Cornelia Corwin the music teacher "Mr. Van Horne's very accomplished teacher."[12]

The people of Fayetteville were proud of their educational institutions and the people who led them. The main families of town supported each and all of them, contributing time, money, land and students whenever they could.

There was a full and diverse Christian community in Fayetteville in 1860. Two of the three schools were run by ministers, with William Baxter of the Christian Church administering Arkansas College and Baptist minister Thomas Van Horne over the Fayetteville Female Institute. Mercus Feemster was a clergyman of the Cumberland Presbyterian Church and associated with the Female Seminary where his two daughters taught. In addition, the Methodists had a resident minister named Richard Hannah, who had a congregation of about fifty-eight people who met in a "modest frame building."[13] The Catholics also had a church organization but not a full-time clergyman.

The people of town, of course, went various directions on Sunday. Probably the largest denomination in town in 1860 was the Christian Church, whose members were called Campbellites. Its founder, Pastor Graham, still lived in town. The local group included Pastor Baxter, with a nucleus of such families as those of Dr. Thomas Jefferson Pollard, store merchant J. Harvey Stirman, and attorneys Wilburn Reagan and Lafayette Gregg. Just a year before, in 1859, they had constructed their own church building. The Baptists organized in June 1858 under Van Horne, and had adherents such as John Buie, Clara Watson and Amanda Peer. They likely met at the Female Institute which Van Horne headed.

Though the population was small, the literate people of frontier Fayetteville were able to support a newspaper. *The Arkansian*, a weekly, issued its first edition on March 5, 1859, under the ownership of attorneys James R. Pettigrew and Elias C. Boudinot. It was "a six-column folio," meaning that it was one large sheet folded in half, then again in half, making four pages total. The purpose of the paper was political in nature, as it expressly stated, "to advance the principles of the Democratic Party, and stay the onrushing tide of abolitionism which threatens the South; to advocate the building of a railroad from the Atlantic to the Pacific, and to secure its location on, or near, the thirty-fifth parallel, and to promote the cause of education."[14] Boudinot, whose family had considerable influence in the Cherokee Nation, also used the paper at times to dabble in Cherokee politics.

"Lay aside your fears that your editor will get rich fasteer than his neighbors," Boudinot wrote in the premiere issue. "We never head of a man making more than a decent living by the publishing of a county newspaper." The paper came out on Fridays until June 16, 1860, and thereafter on Saturdays, and grew to a circulation of some two thousand.[15]

William Quesenberry (pronounced "Cushenberry") was persuaded to be the editor of *The Arkansian*. Known as "Bill Cush," he was perhaps the most colorful person in town. He was an editor, a writer, a political cartoonist, a Mexican War veteran, and an adventurer. When California gold fever swept the nation, he crossed the desert in an unsuccessful pursuit of riches, eventually returning home to Fayetteville. Goodspeed's history wrote that "he was a racy and vigorous writer, an accomplished editor and something of a humorist and poet."[16] Early 20th century writer William S. Campbell said that he "was in many respects the most many-sided man Fayetteville has had for a citizen."[17] From 1854 to 1856 Quesenberry had published his own newspaper in town, *The Southwest Independent*. He and his wife, Adeline, had five children aged two through eleven, and seven slaves.

William Quesenberry ("Bill Cush"). Shiloh Museum.

Quesenberry drew pictures of the Arkansas College and the Fayetteville Female Seminary. When merchant James Van Hoose was married on a stormy night in 1857, Quesenberry published a verse in his honor. "The night was dark and fearful, The thunders made a racket, When James Van Hoose was married, By Rev. Mr. Hackett." In another verse in another poem ended with the phrase, "God loves not him that loves not Arkansas!"[18]

A competing newspaper started in August of 1860 when tailor William W. Moore started *The Fayetteville Democrat*. It's editor was his 21-year-old son, Elias B. Moore, with two other sons, James and William, as printers. Elias was also, since January of that year, the Fayetteville postmaster, distributing the letters brought into town by the Butterfield Overland Stage. The post office was located on the northwest corner of town square. Josiah Washburn, 39, was also listed in the census as an editor.

The economy of Arkansas, like the rest of the country, was based upon agriculture. The professionals and artisans clustered in town, while the farmers lived almost everywhere land could be cultivated. Several farmers were counted by the census within the city limits of Fayetteville, some owning land and others not owning any real estate. The size of the farms owned is not revealed in the census, but the value is recorded. This number is one offered by the owner and may or may not have been accurate, but probably does give some indication of the relative size of the farms. No one in or around Fayetteville had anything like a stereotypical South Carolina cotton plantation, but some of them did have slaves working the land side by side with the farmers.

Three families who identified themselves as farmers in the census were well ahead of others in the value of the land. Charles and Melinda Houghs, aged 46 and 38, respectively, asserted ownership of $17,000 in real estate and $20,000 in personal property. Their five children ranged in age from ten to twenty-one, all of whom attended school in 1860. They owned eighteen slaves, the third largest number in town.

Second in real estate were the McGarrahs, who have already been mentioned. They valued their real estate at $15,000 but their personal property at only $600. This number is low enough to question its accuracy, but perhaps they were land rich and cash poor. In addition, they owned five slaves. Joseph and Mary Lewis, who had two adult sons still living at home, owned land valued at $12,000, with $9,000 in personal property. They also owned a black family of five, consisting of a man and a woman about thirty years old, and three children, ages 6, 4, and 2.

After these three families with large real estate holdings there was a large gap in farm value down to $3,200. Here we find Benjamin and Mary Pegram, formerly of Kentucky and Missouri. They had an interesting juxtaposition of $3,200 in land but a large $15,000 estate in personal property, and no slaves. William and Martha Miller had values of $3,000 and $800, respectively.

Farmers Benjamin and Sallie Gaines listed $3,000 for land and $4,000 for personal property. They had three young children and four slaves. These slaves were a 45-year-old male, 60-year-old and 43-year-old females, and a four year old boy. In other words, one slave worked in the field with one white farmer. It was no plantation.

There was a group of farmers with little land and few personal items. Mathew Leeper had $1,600 and $3,000, with no slaves. Whiting Washington, who had his mother living with him but no family of his own, had $1,200 in land with no listing as to other property. Jacob and Amanda Peer, both at sixty years of age, had just $1,000 in land and a modest $500 in other items. Littleton Graham at 61 had $800 and $1,500 respectively. John and Mary Keller, supporting five children at home, had values of $600 and $100. These people were surely among Fayetteville's poor. "A." and Olivia Bramon of New York had $300 and $150. Jerry and Jane Vertal, Henry and

Margaret Chapman of Ohio, Henry and Ann Shipley of Ohio, Eli and Sarah Fishburn of Ohio, and James and Lucy Henry, all owned no land and had virtually no personal property. These men were likely either farmhands or tenant farmers. They owned no slaves. None of the Northern-born farming families owned any slaves.

Almost everyone was to some extent a farmer. Even people who stated that they had a professional occupation usually had ground upon which they grew crops of some kind. This was true of Jonas Tebbetts, David Walker, and most others.

The census reveals that a wide range of business services were available in Fayetteville in 1860. As might be expected for the day, a number of people were employed in horse and wagon businesses. Charles Butterfield, 24, the son of the owner of the Overland Stage, worked on the stage line and operated a farm west of town. He and his wife, Mary, and their three-year-old daughter Sonia were all born in New York. After arriving in Arkansas, their one-year-old daughter Hattie was born. It is not surprising that with the company owning dozens of stage coaches, that the owner's son and his wife drove a very handsome carriage in town. One of the boarding houses provided lodging for a stage agent (Outsen Bishop), a stage driver (Louis Denton) and two saddlers (Henry Fuver and Prussian-born Richard Gartman).

Henry McRoy had a fairly large carriage shop business. He and his wife, Julia, had two children. Living within their compound were nine men whose occupations were given as blacksmith, carriage tanner, carriage maker and wagon maker. These men were Maurice Coffee, James Parris, George House, Warren House, Albert Fisher and Felen Smith. Running a business meant not only hiring men but often providing a place for them to live as well. He had three more men living with him, Ganet Love, David Dick and a man named Porter, who were all convicts. Whether he housed them as prisoners or as workers is not known.

John Cato was similarly situated but on a smaller scale. He was a blacksmith owning his home and grounds, and had living with him two other men, William Bowers and William Elliott, listed as wagon makers.

In addition, living on their own were another carriage maker (Absalom Bills), five wagon makers (Martin Bonhome, Daniel B. Jobe at the corner of College and Mountain, Leroy Lancaster, Asmus Outzen, Isaac Williams), eight blacksmiths (James Churchwell, Alexander Diester, Solomon Duncan, Robert Hogan, John Lewis, Jonathan Osburne, John Thomas, Clinton Tifanaur), two saddlers (Randolph Calfry and Jefferson Dunlap), and one hostler (horse tender, Robert Blake). It is not surprising that in the 19th century these men constituted a significant portion of Fayetteville's economy with approximately 16% of the adult male labor force engaged in the horse and wagon business.

In a world where most things were made of wood, carpenters were in abundance. One carpenter claiming the unlikely name of Forrest Woods had his sons Richard and John working with him. Another carpenter was Thomas Williford, with his sons Henry, Nelson and Seneca working at his side. Other carpenters included Whitson Taylor, S.M. Ward (who lived at Isaac Taylor's Byrnside's Hotel), Martin Frazier and his son, John, John Fletcher, and Ira Cleveland. George Riley with his family, and Hugh Boswell with his, worked as carpenters and lived together in a single residence. So also with John Brandenburg and John Peer and their families. Americus Rieff, surely used some of his seven slaves in his carpentry work, which was commonly done. Carpenter Edward Peer, his wife and two children, lived with his parents on their farm.

Similarly, cabinet makers provided their services. John Blakeley, who lived with his wife Elizabeth Jane, and their children, Albert and Leonora, was a "cabinet workman" according to the census. Edward Stigowest, Edward Dawson and John Buie claimed the same profession. Not far behind the woodworkers were the plasterers (Roger Fox and Hugh Glass) and then the painters (Charles Hauptmann and Amos Stafford).

A number of men declared their professions to be that of "merchant." These were generally the business owners, large and small. William McIlroy operated a mercantile store on the town square. One of the few brick buildings in town was located on the northeast corner of the square and belonged to merchant Stephen K. Stone. Other merchants included brothers William and Frank Watson, Washington Wilson, Henry Rieff, Stephen Beauford, James Van Horne, Thomas Pollard, Jr., James Stirman, Joseph Holcomb, William Quarles, James Macy, James Sutton, William White, Elijah Davidson and Joseph L. Dickson.

There were six dry goods stores in 1852, and presumably that many or more eight years later. Dickson and Stirman owned a steam mill to grind grain, which was located southeast of town. Addison Crouch had a carding factory, which could card one hundred pounds of wool per day.* It was originally powered by a treadmill with horses and mules, but later he installed a seven horsepower steam engine brought in by wagon from Missouri.[19]

It takes a lot of services to make a town work well. Occupations included butcher (Samuel Binner), bakers (Joseph Zellieh, William Henry), grocers (James Barnes, John Cate, James T. Sutton), shoemakers (Jacob Battenfield, James Carlile, Joshua Carlile, John Ruth), tailors (John Morrow, John Purkins, John Ramsey), seamstress (Elizabeth Casey), animal stock trader (James Jackson), tinsmiths (James Voorhees, Henry Calfry, William Calfry, Amos Choran, Bradburn Jordan, James Pyeatt), nurseryman (James Whitmore), printers (William Smith, Thomas Hines, William Moore, James Moore), watchmakers (Henry D. Ford, Edward E. Pratt, Thomas Rollins, Henry Van Dyke), book agent (Robert Boals), millers (Daniel Jones, Ebeneezer White), millwright (George Smith), gardener (Richard Gannett), tobacconist (Columbus Jackson, who operated a tobacco factory at the corner of Spring and Block Streets), tobacco roller (Robert Harrell), and machinist (James Smith). Other jobs listed in the census included clerks, "labourers," servants, a "U.S. Officer" (George Clark) and a "pedler" from Italy who was staying at the Byrnside's Hotel.

One of the more interesting occupations was that of "ambrotype artist," or in other words, a photographer. There was only one such artisan listed in the census of 1860, and that was Martha Henry. She was 32 years old, a Kentuckian by birth, and apparently childless, as the census listed no children. She was married to William Henry, who was a baker at the grocery of Elmore Cooper. They lived with Cooper and his wife.

Ambrotype photography was a variation of the original daguerreotype, although the actual method of production was quite different. It consisted of creating an image by under-exposing a chemical called collodion on a glass negative, which was then bleached

---

Carding is the process of running raw wool through rollers and wire bristles, straightening and untangling the wool to get it ready for use as clothing material.

and a black background placed behind it. This produced a photograph. The exposure time was shorter than that needed for daguerreotypes, and production was cheaper and quicker. Perhaps it was Martha Henry who created many of the images we have today of the early people of Fayetteville.

The Fayetteville medical community consisted of two long time and several newer doctors. The senior medical practitioners in Fayetteville were two brothers from Kentucky. Dr. Thomas Jefferson Pollard, 54, had graduated with a medical degree at Transylvania University in Lexington in 1828. He had been in town for more than twenty years and was the dean of the profession. By 1860 his children were grown, although his 22-year-old son John and his 18-year-old daughter Ann still lived at home. Also living in the home was 16-year-old Rebecca Stirman, the niece of his wife, Mary. Their son, Thomas Pollard, 27, worked as a merchant in town, living with his wife and two-year-old son. Dr. Pollard's brother Wade, 48, was also a doctor in town, and they practiced medicine together. He and his wife, Emily, had seven children living at home between the ages of 12 and 26.

"Dr. Thomas J. Pollard was the family physician," wrote Marian Tebbetts. "He was a man of education, high culture and unsullied character, a graduate of reputable colleges; he was regarded the most learned physician of northwest Arkansas. Patients came to him from far and near."[20]

The newest medical practices belonged to Dr. James Stevenson, 30, Dr. George Taylor, 29, Dr. Thomas Uncary, 29, and Dr. David Smithson, a 25-year-old young man born and raised in Arkansas. Another physician who lived in the Fayetteville area but was not recorded in the census was Samuel R. Bell, who had been in town for more than ten years, had an office on Main Street. Dr. J. G. Scarborough had an office in his home across the street from the Stephen Stone residence.

Dental services were provided by 25-year-old James Perkins, who lived with, and probably practiced in the office of, Dr. Wade Pollard. Thirty-year-old John R. Palmer, who was apparently living in a hotel or boarding house, had an office on the south side of town square. R.B. Kice had a dental office next to the telegraph office.

The first drug store in town was in 1854 with Dr. James Stevenson.[21] Druggist Frank Paddock came to Fayetteville in the late

1850s. His arrival was remembered by young Marian Tebbetts, the daughter of Jonas and Matilda. "Drugs were furnished by physicians," she wrote many years later, "but along toward the end of the decade someone set up a drugstore. No one supposed it would live, but the druggist added a soda-fount and provided plenty of 'ju-ju' paste, a sweet jellied concoction of some kind that set the young people crazy. Besides, everybody both young and old had to taste the unheard of soda-water, and so the drugstore lived."[22] Paddock, 36, and his 28-year-old wife Mary, were born in New York and New Hampshire, respectively.

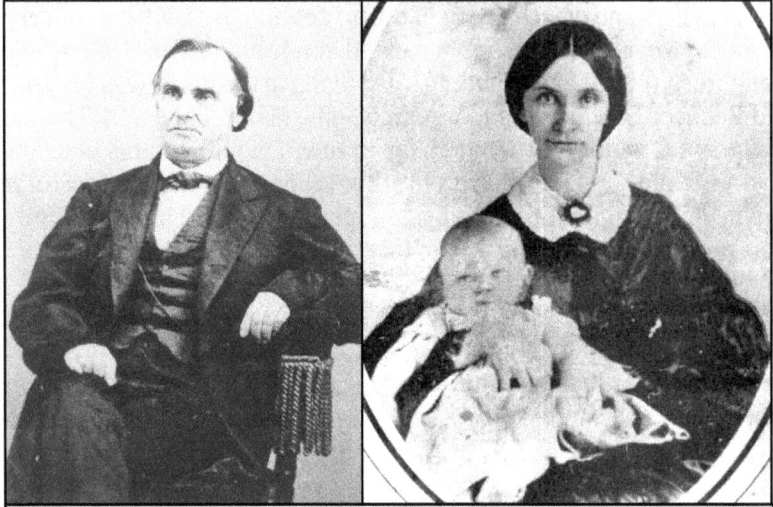

Judge David Walker and his daughter Mary, holding her son Vol. Mary married attorney James David Walker. Waiting for news of an expected battle in Missouri, she was in a state of great anxiety for the safety of her husband. Shiloh Museum.

Fayetteville had an influential legal fraternity in the years before the war. The most eminent of member was 54-year-old David Walker, who had lived in town but in 1860 lived just south of the city limits. After coming to Arkansas from Kentucky in 1830 he was immediately successful. Walker was a delegate to the Arkansas Constitutional Convention in 1836, a Whig candidate for Congress in 1844 (losing to Archibald Yell), and a member of the Arkansas Supreme Court from 1848 to 1855. He resigned in 1855 and returned home to Fayetteville. His wife, Jane, had died in 1847, apparently in childbirth, and he raised six children as a widower.*

His son-in-law and cousin, James David Walker, was also practicing law in town. He was 29 years old, having come from Kentucky in 1847. He studied at the Ozark Institute of Robert Mecklin, studied law with David Walker, and was admitted to the bar in 1850. In 1857 he married Judge Walker's daughter, Mary, making her Mary Walker Walker.

Wilburn D. Reagan, 44, came to Fayetteville in 1838 and practiced law. "He was excessively aggressive," reported Goodspeed's history in 1889, "and was wont to rely for success upon sarcasm and invective, and his ability to browbeat witnesses and overawe juries, rather than upon a knowledge of the law and skillful presentation of his case."[23]

For about the last eight years he had practicing with him a bachelor named James R. Pettigrew. He had been an 1850 graduate of Arkansas College. His legal style was different from that of Reagan. "He was never eloquent but was a fine reasoner," it was said later, "and the plain blunt way of stating his ideas carried conviction to his hearers and he was ever regarded as one of the best practitioners at the Fayetteville bar."[24] He lived with his widowed mother, Sarah Pettigrew.

Alfred M. Wilson was a 43-year-old attorney in 1860, a descendant of a signer of the Declaration of Independence, James Wilson. He had been a state prosecutor during the 1840s, and since 1853 was the U.S. attorney for the western district of Arkansas. He had been a member of the Arkansas legislature frm 1848 to 1852. His wife, Isabella, died in 1857, perhaps in childbirth, and he lived as a widower with his four sons, aged three to ten. He was one of the major slave owners in town, with nineteen.

---

* Archibald Yell was the most famous of Fayetteville's residents before the Civil War. He was a Congressman, Governor and General, who was killed at the Battle of Buena Vista in the Mexican War. His original law office is now preserved by the Washington County Historical Society on the site of Headquarters House, 118 East Dickson, in Fayetteville.

Jonas Tebbetts, right, with a Union officer. Born in New England, he moved to the South as a young man and became a slave owner. Twenty years in Arkansas could not override his loyalty to the Union. Shiloh Museum.

Jonas M. Tebbetts, 40, was the only Northern-born attorney in town, having come from New Hampshire. However, at the age of twenty he moved to Van Buren, Arkansas, where he began his career. He was elected to the legislature 1846 and 1848. He moved to Fayetteville to be legal counsel for the Bank of Arkansas, and in 1850 he was again elected to the legislature, this time from Washington County. He was co-owner of a large grain mill with Stirman and Dickson. His wife Matilda was a grand-niece of James Madison and a relative of Zachary Taylor. They owned two slaves in 1860. The Tebbetts family lived in a house on a four acre lot at the northeast corner of town at the intersection of the Old Missouri Road and the Telegraph Road, now designated as 118 East Dickson and is the long time home of the Washington County Historical Society.

Lafayette Gregg, 35, who had studied law with Reagan, was currently the criminal prosecutor in the Fourth Circuit. Born in Alabama, he came to Arkansas at the age of ten and went to the Ozark Institute. He was briefly a teacher, then turned to law and served for a time in the state legislature. He lived with his wife, Mary, and their two young sons.

Thomas M. Gunter, 33, came to town as a young man in 1853 and studied law. He married and had a son, Julius, but his wife soon died. He married again, this time to Jennie Bragg. She was a relative of Braxton Bragg, who later became a Confederate general. In 1860 they had not yet had any children of their own, though they still had Julius with them. They lived on the north end of town.

Other attorneys were Peter Van Hoose, Lafayette Boone, 25, who grew up west of town, 23-year-old William Vaney and 33-year-old John Wilson. Mathew Leeper was an attorney who had been sent to Arkansas by President Andrew Jackson to be a receiver in the land office, but had never actively practiced in the profession. He was always an ardent Jacksonian Democrat.

Some of the Washington County government officials lived in the county seat of Fayetteville. Presley Smith, who had previously been the sheriff for four years, had been elected County Clerk every two years starting in 1846, and he was still in office in 1860. Smith had two deputy court clerks, 18-year-old Martin S. Hawkins and 17-year-old James Henrie. Sheriff John Crawford lived with his wife, Mary, and their four children. Leroy Cunningham was the recorder at the land office.

The census taker generally listed the man's name first when taking family information, and would list his occupation. Then his wife would be listed, and no occupation would generally be stated. Older sons also had their occupations listed, but not daughters. No one need suppose, however, that William Miller and his 20-year-old son George, who were listed as farmers, but 38-year old wife and mother Martha and 18-year-old daughter Elizabeth were just as much farmers as the men regardless of what the census enumerator may say. All would have carried their share of the work on a frontier farm.

Nor did single women who were heads of households have their occupations listed. There were not many of these. Isabella Sutton's husband Seneca Sutton died in 1857, so she was listed first in the census without an occupation. Her 18-year-old son Henry, who lived with her along with three other children, was listed as a clerk. Her adult son James was married and lived next door. Jane Hawkins, 55, headed her house and owned three slaves. The two spaces beneath her name on the census form were, for reasons now unknown, left blank, but it is known that her son, Martin Hawkins, was listed with his employer, Presley Smith.

Elizabeth Barrington, who had a husband in the 1850 census, had none in 1860 and so was presumably a widow. She lived with her four children plus an additional 15-year-old girl. No occupation is stated for her. So also with Cynthia Smithson and her four children between the ages of 17 and 28, Margaret Pope and children aged 16 to 29, and Martha Heath and her 17-year-old son. Martha Henry, the ambrotype artist, was the only married woman in town who had a profession attributed to her.

Sarah Arrington, 44, seems to have been the only divorced woman in Fayetteville. She had been married to Alfred W. Arrington, an attorney and one-time Methodist minister who was expelled from the church and accused of adultery. Alfred "was very erratic in his manner of living, and lacked mental balance. He frequently indulged in fits of dissipation, and did many things to destroy the confidence of the public in him."[25] After his Methodist ministry he became a preaching infidel, ultimately renouncing his apostasy and becoming a minister again. He became a lawyer and was elected to the legislature. He was a Whig presidential elector in 1844 but voted straight Democratic that year except for David Walker, the Whig candidate for Congress. Alfred left his wife and children for Texas, reportedly taking his mistress with him, and never saw his family again.[26]

Sarah divorced him about 1845. Fifteen years later the two youngest of the four children, 20-year-old Alfred Jr. and 17-year-old Annette, were still living with her. Also in the home was the oldest daughter, 25-year-old Mary Arrington Strickland, one of the first graduates of the Fayetteville Female Institute. She had her own children, aged six and four, and she was apparently a widow.

Single women, however, were listed in the census with their occupations. The female teachers, who all lived with other families, are listed above. In 1860 Elizabeth Casey, forty years old and a seamstress, was the only single woman in Fayetteville living alone in her own separate residence.

The Fayetteville citizens with a connection to the people for whom the county and city were named were Rebecca Washingon and her son, Whiting Washington. Washington County, of course, was named in honor of George Washington, and Fayetteville. His trusted general, the Marquis de Lafayette, toured America in the 1820s and had several cities named for him throughout the country.[*] Rebecca,

---

Fayette in Alabama, Mississippi, Missouri, New York, and Ohio. Fayetteville in Arkansas, Georgia, New York, North Carolina, Pennsylvania, Tennessee, and Virginia (now West Virginia). Lafayette in Georgia, Indiana, Iowa, Louisiana, Minnesota, New York, Ohio, and Tennessee.

who was 74 years old in 1860 and the oldest person in town, was the living link to these names.

Rebecca Smith had married Whiting Washington, whose father Warner was a cousin of George Washington. By that time "the father of his country" was already dead. Her husband had since died, and she lived as a widow with her son, Whiting Washington Jr., who was a blood relative of the first President. Rebecca was the mother-in-law of Judge David Walker andf grandmother of Mary Walker. Her sister, Lucy Smith, also lived in Fayetteville in 1860.[27]

Rebecca Washington, whose deceased husband was a remote cousin of George Washington. Washington County Historical Society.

The people of Fayetteville of necessity provided their own entertainment, mostly through their churches, schools and the masonic lodge. The lodge was organized in 1835, reportedly the first one in Arkansas. It was located at the northwest corner of Block and Rock Streets in a two-story framed building constructed five years later. Many of the men in town were involved in the fraternity, including Mathew Leeper, Washington Wilson, J. Harvey Stirman, William R. Quarles, Jonas M. Tebbetts, Robert Graham, Peter Van Hoose, and many others.

Entertainments were what the people themselves made. "In a small town where there are no public diversions, save going to church," recalled Marian Tebbetts, "the inhabitants have to make their own amusements. Picnics, dances, charades, tableaus [plays], and in winter, when there is snow enough, sleigh rides, the sleighs manufactured out of wagon beds set on runners, and other innocent things."[28]

The first Washington County Fair was held in town square in the fall of 1856. Winning exhibits were displayed in the courthouse in the center of the square, and races and livestock shows were held in the streets. Starting the next year a fairground was established just south of town for the annual event.[29]

Some diversions did come from out of town. New people to talk to and get news from came in wagon trains. Marian Tebbetts said "it was a common thing to see covered wagons trailing through the town" heading west.[30] With the coming of the Overland Stage came more visitors, newspapers and letters.

Mabrie's Menagerie and Circus came to Fayetteville on May 21, 1859. It featured the first elephant brought to northwest Arkansas, clowns, and horse shows. *The Arkansian* reported that the circus played to "crowded houses."[31] Other traveling shows also made their appearances.

As was common throughout the 18th and 19th centuries, a local militia was organized in Washington County. However, it fell into disuse and was inactive until 1860. The 20th Regiment of the Arkansas Militia was rejuvenated by Henry Rieff, a 36-year-old merchant in Fayetteville. He was appointed colonel of the regiment, and in January reported to Governor Elias N. Conway that "the militia of this regiment have not done any duty for several years and I do not know who are officers and who are not. Some have died.... I shall proceed at once to have this regiment officered and enrolled and I think the times and signs of the times favor it."[32] This comment, of course, referred to the dark political clouds that hinted at possible civil war.

Rieff immediately raised a militia company in Fayetteville with George C. North as captain, J.W. Walker first lieutenant, William D. Smithson second lieutenant, and James H. Van Hoose third lieutenant. The company named itself "the Washington Rifle Guards." The next month the "Washington County Mounted Rifles" were formed as another company. This was officered by Captain James M. Tuttle, First Lieutenant Peter Van Hoose, 2nd Lieutenant William R. Cunningham and Third Lieutenant James R. Pettigrew. Another battalion was organized south of town, with Thomas J. Hunt as Captain of Company G, Thomas Gilstrap as Captain of Company H, and George W.M. Reed as Captain of Company E.

Births, marriages and deaths, as always, were an everyday occurrence. According to the census, within the twelve months from July 1859 to July 1860, seventeen babies were born to the residents of Fayetteville. Also, three 17-year-old girls were married: Mary to 28-

year-old James Bams, Ann to 25-year-old John Brandenburg, and Martha to 28-year-old William Smithson.

During the last year death had taken its inevitable toll. On November 16, 1859, Kate Wilson, the wife of merchant Washington Wilson, died "after an illness of over eight months." On April 7, 1860, Margaret Byrnside, a Fayetteville pioneer and co-founder of Byrnside's Hotel, died. Her funeral was conducted by Pastor Baxter, who all too soon had his own loss. On August 18, 1860, William and Fidelia Baxter lost their young son Harry, aged one year and twenty-six days.

In August of 1860 William L. Quarles passed away. The *Arkansian* reported a large attendance at his funeral. On October 4, 1860, young Harry Tebbetts, son of Jonas and Matilda Tebbetts, died at the age of a year and a half. His sister Marian said that the cause of his passing was "summer complaint,"[33] now known as crib death.

Slavery

Fayetteville, like all Southern towns, was a community of harsh contrasts. Nearly a third of its citizens were enslaved and lived impoverished and restricted lives. It is beyond the scope of this book to analyze the causes and effects of slavery. What can a 21st century person say in defense of such an institution? Perhaps all that can be said is that things were different then - incomprehensibly different. How otherwise good and decent white people would consent to own black people is something not now to be fully understood. Neither is the endless indignity that slavery heaped upon African people.

Yet it was so. Not only did the Southern people of Fayetteville, who were raised in a society steeped in bondage, participate in the practice, but so also did Northern-born people. Jonas Tebbetts of New Hampshire, who had a Southern wife, owned two slaves in 1860. English-born Pastor William Baxter owned five slaves, which perhaps were attributable to his position as president of the Arkansas College.

To say that some people did own slaves is not to subtract from their character their individual virtues. Good and kindly people were in fact good and kindly people. The reconciliation of these virtues with slavery is what now is an impossible task. There was a mind set then that is a stranger to us now.

It is no surprise, though nonetheless unfortunate, that the people who were enslaved in Fayetteville left little by way of written record. The story of 30% of the townspeople during the Civil War would be more fully told here if it were more fully known. The reader is asked to bear in mind that there is an untold story that accompanies the one that is told.

Slavery was a fact in mid-nineteenth century America, and Arkansas was a slave state from the beginning. There were no free blacks in 1860 because a recent state law required all such people to leave Arkansas. The geography of northwest Arkansas was not suitable for plantations so most of the slaves in the area were house servants, farm hands or workers such as carpenters.

The 1860 census did take a count of slaves, but not in the same manner as with the whites. It did not list them by name, but rather individually by owner. For each slave the age, sex and color (black or mulatto) were recorded. Also, the number of "slave houses" per owner was asked. Slaves in town generally lived in cabins in the back yards of the white homes. According to the slave schedules for Fayetteville, there were 294 slaves in 1860. This constituted 30% of the total population, which was a little higher than the 26% of Arkansas as a whole.

Fayetteville was the sixth largest city in the state but had the fourth highest number of slaves. It averaged well more slaves per slaveowner than the state average of four. "The townhouses of wealthy Arkansas slaveowners were staffed with a variety of house servants.... Slaves worked in the hotels, boarding houses, and taverns of the towns.... Town slaves were also known to have worked as draymen [cart drivers], garden-plowmen, house painters, house movers, and street laborers. Much of the street repair in the incorporated towns was done by slaves...."[34]

The largest slave owner living within the city limits of Fayetteville in 1860 was Byrnside's Hotel keeper Isaac Taylor, who owned 32. They lived in ten slave houses, which was far more than the usual. Perhaps they resided in a wing of the hotel. These people were remarkably young. Five were under a year old; 21 were under 20. The oldest was a forty-five year old female, none were in their thirties. Ten were in their 20s. Their average age was 13.6 years. The oldest slaves in town were two 60-year-olds.

Fayetteville in the Civil War

Some of Fayetteville's ex-slaves posing for the camera many years later. Willis Pettigrew, Sam Van Winkle, Charlie Richardson, Squire Fahagen, and Nick Clemmons.
Washington County Historical Society.

This youthfulness was a pattern that held true throughout the slave population of Fayetteville. Alfred M. Wilson and Charles Houghs were tied for second in the number of slaves at nineteen each. Of these 38 people, the oldest was 35. A total of five were in their 30s, seven in their 20s, and 26 were nineteen and under. The average age was 14.6 years.

Some slaves were listed as being owned by women. Jane Hawkins, the head of her household, owned three slaves, aged 30, 8 and 4. Susan Inger, apparently a widow living with her daughter and her husband, owned an 18-year-old male slave, while her son-in-law Benjamin Gaines owned four more. Margaret Pope, the head of her household of three children, owned seven slaves. In the William Quarles family, one slave was owned by the father, but the ownership of four and three slaves are respectively attributed to Mary and Martha, who were in their mid-twenties and apparently nieces of William.

"Generally speaking," wrote Marian Tebbetts, "the negroes about Fayetteville were humanely treated. Occasionally, unheard of stories trickled in, and once a big, strong negro woman died very suddenly, and was just as suddenly buried." Of course, Marian was a young white girl who knew nothing of the horrors of slavery.

Yet even she acknowledges the black people of Fayetteville lived in fear. The ugly fact is that slavery must be based upon violence and fear to enforce the system upon the subjugated people. When slaves became too numerous, she said, "the 'nigger trade' took the surplus off south and sold them. Nothing was more abhorrent to the average Negro than the 'nigger trader' and the patrolers - usually pronounced 'patterrollers....' There were times when the patrolers were more vigilant than others - when no Negro dared go on the street at night without a pass from his master."

Marian's mother, Matilda Tebbetts, wrote a letter to husband Jonas who was in Little Rock on business. "The patrolers gave me a fright last night," she said, "by stopping before my window and letting their light shine in..... I don't think it right that the whole town should be disturbed because [Wilburn] Reagan's Negroes ran off. He found his Negroes in Ft. Smith and it gave him a spite at all the Negroes in town."[35]

Adeline Blakely was a young slave owned by John Parkes, who was deeded to Parkes's daughter, Elizabeth, when she married John Blakely.

The patrolers were well remembered many years later by Adeline, who had been a slave girl of the John Blakeley family.* She was ten years old in 1860 and owned by John P.A. Parks. "It was a custom to give a girl a slave when she was married," she said. "When Miss Parks became Mrs. Blakeley she moved to Fayetteville and chose me to take with her."[36]

"Yes, we were afraid of the patyroles," Adeline recalled. "All colored folks were. They said that any Negroes that were caught away from their master's premises without a permit would be whipped by the patyroles. They used to sing a song: 'Run nigger run, the patyroles will get you.'"[37]

Notwithstanding their fear, slaves did sometimes run away in

---

* After the war she took the surname of Blakeley, and stayed with the family until her death in 1945.

hope of freedom. Frederick Douglass, perhaps the most famous runaway slave in the nation, escaped from his Maryland plantation to freedom in the North. It has been attributed to him that he said to an audience later that "I appear before you this evening as a thief and a robber. I stole this head, these limbs, this body, from my master, and ran off with them."

Deed to a Slave.

"Know all whom it may concern that...I, John P.A. Parkes of the County of Washington in the State of Arkansas for an in consideration of the natural love and affection which I have for my daughter Elizabeth J. Blakeley (wife of John Blakeley of the City of Fayetteville in Arkansas)....I have this day given, bargained, sold and conveyed...my negro girl slave for life, about nine years old and named Adeline.... It witness whereof I have hereunto set my hand...this 18th day of January, AD 1861.
John P.A. Parks."

Washington County resident Alfred Wallace owned a slave by the name of Nelson Hacket, who worked as a valet and butler. While Wallace was away to another part of the state in July 1841, Hacket stole Wallace's horse, a watch, a coat and a saddle belonging to Fayetteville merchant Washington L. Wilson. He fled all the way to freedom in Canada, but the slave hunters devised on an ingenious plan to bring him back. Canada would not return runaway slaves, but Hacket was indicted in the Fayetteville court for grand larceny in the theft of the horse and saddle, and criminal extradition was demanded by Governor Archibald Yell. The Canadian authorities ordered that he be returned, which caused an international incident. The Prime Minister in London, who still governed Canada, decreed that fugitive slaves would never again be turned over for criminal violations.[38]

In 1856 a descendant of Daniel Boone, Dr. James Boone, 67, a widower living about five miles from town in an area now called Elkins, was murdered. Boone was one of the first physicians in the area, had been a delegate to the Arkansas Constitutional Convention in 1836, and was popular and well known. Three slaves, two of whom belonged to Boone and one to a neighbor, were arrested. "Fayetteville the next day was the scene of a milling mob which congregated on the dirt streets and clustered in little knots about the jail steps."[39] One of the sons of Dr. Boone led the mob into the jail, brought out the two slaves and hanged them. The third one was tried and also hanged.

This is an interesting proposition, that one could hang one's own slaves with impunity, but another's slave must be tried before the "property" can be taken from its owner and hanged. Due process was accorded the owner of the third slave because he was losing property, but not to the slave himself Dr. Boone had three sons. They were, in order of age, Ewlar, Benjamin and Lafayette. Which did the hanging is not known. In 1860 Benjamin and Lafayette were young attorneys in Fayetteville.

In 1860 a man named Mullis living in nearby Mountain Township was murdered by his slave, who pled self defense. The slave was held in jail in Fayetteville, but a mob from Mountain Township came and hanged him. This is probably the incident that Marian Tebbetts referred to in her writings. "Once a mob caught up with a man," she wrote, "who had committed a terrible crime and hanged him, south of town, then cut off his head and hung it on a pole for the buzzards and for a warning. All of which was a terror the children and Negroes."[40] Things were different then.

"We colored folks were not allowed to be taught to read or write," said Adeline Blakeley.[41] At least some of the slaves were permitted to have religious observances. There was reportedly a small building behind the Methodist Church on Center Street, and the Episcopal Church provided a gallery, where the slaves worshiped.

The Presidential Election of 1860

In April 1860 the voters (white males 21 years of age or older) of Fayetteville elected Stephen Bedford as Mayor. The City Council selected was composed of attorney James R. Pettigrew, merchant Joseph Holcomb, stage line operator Charles E Butterfield, merchant James T. Sutton, merchant James H. Van Hoose, and and Dr. Wade T. Pollard.[42] Butterfield and Stirman were holdovers from the previous Council, but the others were new. Attorney Elias C. Boudinot, wool carder Addison Crouch, J.B. Simpson and Mayor J.W. Walker, left office.

The upcoming presidential election cast a pall over the year 1860. With talk of possible disunion and war, political clouds darkened everyone's sky as people thought of the future with deep foreboding. This was as true of Fayetteville as anywhere else in the

United States. The cause of this was the promise by several Southern states that they would secede from the Union if the Republican candidate, Abraham Lincoln, were elected President.

The presidential election reflected the political divisions within society. The Democratic Party, which had for a decade been the chief unifier of the nation, split into factions with two sectional candidates. Vice President John C. Breckinridge of Kentucky was the "Southern rights" candidate, while Senator Stephen A. Douglas of Illinois ran as the moderate reconciliation candidate of the Northern Democrats. The remnants of two fast disappearing political parties, the Whigs and the Know-Nothings, formed the Constitutional Union Party and ran Senator John Bell of Tennessee as a Southern reconciliation candidate. The still-new Republican Party nominated former Congressman Abraham Lincoln of Illinois on a platform of stopping the further spread of slavery.

The Southern extremists could not abide the thought of a "black Republican" President. They threatened that if Lincoln were elected, they would secede before he took office, and would not wait for him to actually do something contrary to their interests. Moderates, who predominated in Arkansas and the Upper South, preferred to wait until Lincoln actually did something before taking the drastic step of disunion.

Presidential candidates at that time did not actively campaign, but rather let their supporters and surrogates go about the country campaigning for them. Lincoln, Breckinridge and Bell followed this tradition, but Douglas, breaking all tradition, became the first to hit the presidential campaign trail.. He felt that the country was going to lapse into division and civil war, and gave all his heart in trying to prevent it. As the only candidate across the entire nation, he traveled the North and South calling for reconciliation.

In Arkansas, Douglas, Breckinridge and Bell all had supporters. Lincoln, having no support in the state, ran no slate of presidential electors and received no votes. Fayetteville was divided among the three candidates, and each had its own vocal adherents.

Fayetteville Attorney Alfred M. Wilson was outspoken in his support of states rights and opposition to Lincoln. He wrote in a letter that "Breck[inridge] was the only candidate in the field...that had the

Alfred M. Wilson was a Whig, but when that party collapsed he became a Southern rights Democrat. He supported John C. Breckinridge for President in 1860. Washington County Historical Society.

honesty and statesmanship to declare in favor of Congressional protection of slave property in our territories - and that Mr D[ouglas] is but the little king of squatterism [i.e., popular sovereignty] and wholly unfit to be trusted by southern people. The southern part of Arkansas is spunky, but the western and northern parts are very inclined to Black Republicanism, and I expect will vote to fold their arms and tamely submit."[43]

This statement of an inclination to "Black Republicanism" is an exaggeration as there was no support for Lincoln anywhere in the state. Rather, Wilson appears to have categorized anyone not at his extreme position as being in the opposite extreme position.

Attorney David Walker, on the other hand, was a long-time moderate Whig, a follower of the great compromiser Henry Clay. In 1836 he had been a presidential elector for Hugh L. White, who was the Southern Whig candidate against Democrat Martin Van Buren. White did not carry Arkansas, however, so Walker never had the opportunity to cast an electoral vote. Now in 1860 he supported Southern moderate and former Whig John Bell of Tennessee for President.

James Van Hoose was also a supporter of Bell. According to Van Hoose, Dr. Thomas Jefferson Pollard, Hugh F. Thomas, Robert W. Mecklin, Mark Bean, Bill Quesenberry, James D. Walker and Zeb M. Pettigrew, were also backers of the Constitutional Union candidate. He said that Alfred M. Wilson, Charles W. Deane and Wilburn Reagan supported Breckinridge.[44] Reagan was a particularly outspoken in his support of Southern states rights.

In support of Bell, Walker and others erected the tallest flagpole yet to appear on top of the courthouse in town square. They got the multi-talented Bill Quisenberry to cut out a tin eagle and star to place on top of it, and unfurled am 18 by 36 foot flag several women in town made for the occasion.

During the campaign an excitement went through Fayetteville when it was announced that Vice President Breckinridge would be coming through town with Senator Milton Latham of California on the Butterfield stage, bound for California. This was to be on Saturday, July 14th, one of the days that Marshal Parks was in town taking the census. Breckinridge was a hero to much of the South, and came from a prominent Kentucky family well known in the border states. Townspeople of all political persuasions were interested in seeing this famous man, and great preparations were made for his reception.

"The day at last arrived and our town was soon full of people of all political parties who had come to town to see a live Vice-President of the United States. Arrangements had been made to entertain our distinguished guests at the Byrnside's Hotel, and a committee, consisting of six gentlemen, had been appointed by a meeting previously held in the courthouse to receive the distinguished gentlemen...and escort them to the courthouse, where they were expected to greet the people.... Several hundred persons were assembled on the streets and a large flag was floating from the flag staff on the cupola of the courthouse and smaller flags from all the business houses around the public square, the anvil batteries[*] were arranged at the corners of the court square and everything in readiness to make a big noise and give to our distinguished visitors a good impression of Arkansas.

"The well-known 'toot toot' of Charley Butterfield's stage horn was heard at the upper end of College Avenue and in a few minutes we saw the big concord coach drawn by four large fine steeds with Charley on the box with lines and whip in hand, turning the corner at the east end of Center Street. The anvil batteries manned by Jim and Dave Stone and Perry Deane were touched off and quickly recharged and fired again and again, while the many hundreds of enthusiastic people shouted and waved their hats, the ladies waving their

---

An "anvil battery" was a means of using an anvil and gunpowder to produce a loud bang similar to the sound of artillery. It was used when a real cannon was not available.

handkerchiefs and parasols at the supposed great man who was leaning out of the window of the stagecoach, return salutation, by waving his hand at the excited multitude, as the foam covered steeds of the gallant Charley Butterfield dashed through the crowd on the public square, and were reined up in front of the Byrnside's Hotel....

"The committee of reception, headed by A.M. Wilson, proceeded at once to the hotel to escort the great Democratic standard bearer of the nation to the courthouse, to be introduced to the people who were anxious to hear a speech from the next President of the United States..... Douglas and Lincoln were also candidates for the same office for which Breckinridge was a candidate but neither one of them had friends enough in this town or county to furnish a representative on this committee of reception.

"When our committee reached the tavern we were greatly disappointed to learn from Senator Latham than Vice-President Breckinridge had changed his program and decided not to accompany him to California.... Senator Latham very kindly consented to represent the Vice-President and make a short speech to our people whose expectations had been raised so high...."[45] This humorous incident was Fayetteville's high point in the presidential election of 1860.

At that time state and national elections were not simultaneously held. In September the state and local elections were held. Lafayette Gregg ran for Washington County Prosecuting Attorney and was elected 1,534 to 744 over John R. Cox. Presley Smith was elected for the eighth consecutive time as County Clerk, defeating Zeb Pettigrew 1,424 to 946. Merchant William A. Watson was elected Treasurer over Joseph Holcomb 978 to 833, and Peter P. Van Hoose was elected school commissioner 1,375 to 739 for Francis M. Smiley. Sheriff John Crawford was not a candidate for re-election as Sheriff, but was elected to the legislature, along with Benjamin F. Boone. D.C. Smithson was defeated for the legislature.[46]

Two months later the voters of Fayetteville and the nation went back to the polls and voted for President. Voting in 1860 was done very differently then. There was no voter registration; people could vote wherever they happened to be on election day. Although voting was done by ballot, it was not considered to be the business of government to provide them. Voters were expected to bring their own ballots, which theoretically required a thoughtful person to sit down beforehand and write out the various offices up for election and the name of the persons for whom he was voting.

Reality was a bit different from that, however. Political parties were quick to save a voter the trouble of writing anything down, and had ballots printed up beforehand with all of the offices listed along with the names of that party's candidates. Party newspapers, surely including *The Arkansian* and *The Fayetteville Democrat*, printed ballots that could be used, but if one missed it, political workers would be outside the polling places, offering the arriving voters their respective party ballots. There was no real secrecy in voting because these ballots were usually printed in distinctive colors for all to see which ticket was being voted.

Washington County was closely divided between Breckinridge and Bell, the former winning by only a plurality. The peace candidates

---

1860 Presidential Election

	United States		Arkansas		Washington County	
Lincoln	1,855,276	40%	0		0	
Douglas	1,004,042	21%	5,390	10%	244	11%
Breckinridge	672,601	14%	28,732	53%	1,028	48%
Bell	590,980	13%	20,096	37%	881	41%
Anti-Lincoln*	553,570	12%	0		0	

* The Douglas, Breckenridge and Bell supporters in New York, New Jersey and Pennsylvania ran a single coalition or "fusion," ticket against Lincoln, which received the votes indicated. No fusion ticket ran Arkansas. (Michael J. Dubin, *United States Presidential Elections 1788-1860* (Jefferson, N.C.: McFarland Company, 2002), pp. 159-160.)

---

of Bell and Douglas, taken together, provided a majority. Arkansas as a whole gave a slight majority to Breckinridge.

Nationally, however, the voting was very much different. With the anti-Lincoln vote divided three ways, it was a virtual certainty that Lincoln would win. He swept the Northern states which, with their greater population, produced an electoral majority for the Republicans. With his inauguration as President set for March 4, 1861, the nation waited to see whether the Southern extremists would actually take the threatened step of secession.

Once it was known that Lincoln had won, politics became the topic of the day, every day. *The Arkansian* did not believe that the South should secede immediately, but rather wait until President-elect Lincoln actually did something against the South. Then, it said on November 24, 1860, if Lincoln did do something then the people should "impeach him, damn him and damn him forever."[47] Obviously, feelings were running very high.

Matthew Leeper, who was out of town, wrote a letter on November 29th to Judge Walker. He predicted the future more accurately that he could have known or desired. "No man can reasonably anticipate the desolation which would ensue," Leeper wrote of secession. "Civil war would be the inevitable consequence, neighbor would be arrayed in arms against his neighbor, brother against brother and father against his son, until in after years we would look back with despairing mockery and utter ruin, which our folly have brought upon us. In meeting such a fearful crisis the odds in every particular is against the South... I am not an alarmist and believe that I am speaking nothing but the truth"[48] He was, indeed.

It did not take long for the suspense to end as Southern governors issued calls for state secession conventions to meet. On December 20, 1860, South Carolina met first and passed an ordinance of secession. On New Year's Eve the people of Fayetteville could only guess what might become of themselves and their town.

1861
Confederate Days

"We have established ourselves free and independent."

The political division of families began immediately. Judge David Walker of Fayetteville and his sister, Emily Walker Wheeler, quickly fell into a quarrel over secession. Emily wrote from Texas on January 15, 1861, that "I should greatly admire your truly patriotic sentiments and your devotion to the Union if there was any longer a union to preserve. Why would you embalm the dead body when the spirit has fled? ...You pray for blessings on Sam Houston*.... I advise you to pray again...for perhaps your god is asleep or on a journey."

"You have written a very foolish letter to me," David shot back in a reply. "You know nothing of the political difficulties that beset us, save what you may have caught up from reckless assertions of politicians and papers." Trying to take the sting out of their differences, he said, "As to your indirect allusions to my position in politics as traitorous to my country, and my remarks in reply, I assure you that I felt not at all sensitive upon my own account."[49] They tried to look past their political difficulties, both speaking instead of the health of various family members and friends, but it was nonetheless an unhappy battle between brother and sister.

On January 24, 1861, the Arkansas legislature called for an election to determine whether a secession convention should be held and, if so, who should be the delegates. This seriously heightened political tensions. People had to decide whether they were for secession or for the Union, and positions became radicalized.

The next day *The Fayetteville Arkansian* carried a letter to the public written by Benjamin F. Boone, a representative from Washington County in the Arkansas House of Representatives. On Christmas Eve he had written a letter by Boone that had been published in the *Little Rock True Democrat*. After posing the fact that

---

*Sam Houston was then Governor of Texas and he refused to swear loyalty to the Confederacy after Texas seceded, so was removed from office.

South Carolina had seceded and Alabama and other states were about to, he asked, "Then what, I ask, is Arkansas to do? To fold her arms and look quietly on? Nay! Let her brave sons bestir themselves, meet in convention, lay down an ultimatum to the North which will secure our rights in the Union, and it is acceded to by the North, then Arkansas will hold the proud title attitude of standing as a mediator." He went on to say that should this effort fail "then the tug of war must and will come, and Arkansas will assuredly link her name and her fortunes with her sister southern States...."[50]

On February 2nd a mass meeting of 400 to 500 people was held in Fayetteville. Benjamin F. Boone was chosen chairman, with James H. Van Hoose and M.C. Duke as secretaries. Dr. Thomas J. Pollard read a resolution that had been adopted in Boonsboro a few days earlier: "Resolved, That it is the sense of this meeting that if the efforts of border States, to-wit: Virginia, Maryland, Delaware North Carolina, Tennessee, Kentucky, and Missouri, shall fail to adjust the present political troubles of our country, that the interests of Arkansas being common with theirs, she shall take such action as those of the older and more powerful slave States shall indicate for themselves."

This was a moderate proposition because it favored following the more moderate Upper South states rather than the more radical states of the Lower South. David Walker, merchant James H. Stirman, Dr. George W. Taylor, J.B. Russell and Charles W. Dean declared themselves in favor of this resolution.

Mayor Stephen Bedford then charged that the meeting was fixed by pre-arrangement, that the chairman had been secretly selected a week before and that the secretaries Van Hoose and Duke were secessionists. The meeting then lapsed into confusion and adjourned without resolution of anything.[51] Merchant Stephen K. Stone was not worried. He thought there would be little blood shed in whatever might happen, and left the meeting.[52]

Attorney Alfred M. Wilson thought differently. In a letter from Fayetteville dated February 14, 1861, he recorded how tense things were during the secession winter of 1861. "Everything here is in great excitement (political) and really there is nothing doing except talking politics," he wrote. "What Arkansas will do remains to be seen. But my opinion is we will go out of the union. But so I thought of Ten[nessee] but we learned otherwise last evening. Up to a day or two since I thought there would be no war, but now my mind on that point is changed. I believed that the safety of the South depended upon united action, and that the South would unite in a demand upon the North to recede from their hellish doctrine and respect the federal Constitution & that in default thereon, the South would unite in a Southern Republic. But the silly action of that most silly state of Ten[nessee] having refused even to hold a convention, destroys the last hope for peace. This will...induce the Black Rep[ublican]s of the North to conclude that at least one state in the South will submit to anything and therefore coertion will be resorted to upon Miss[issippi] and other seceding states.... I would be rejoiced at a fair offer of settlement of troubles & hope it may be effected without blood, but I have no faith in it being done."[53]

David Walker questioned the resolve of many of the unionists. "There are a great many up here who profess to be Union men," he wrote on January 29th, "but I find they chuckle and rejoice at every extreme disunion movement. They say they would be for the Union if there was any chance, but time has passed etc. etc. Now, sir, I would greatly prefer open enemies." He said that "it is probable that I will run for the Convention. If I do, or whether I do or not, I will do all im my power to restore peace, and prevent extreme measures in this State. I owe this to posterity and children more than to myself."[54] He did in fact decide to run for the office of secession convention delegate as a unionist.

Should a secession convention be held, Washington County was to select delegates to attend. The unionist candidates, who promised to vote against secession, were attorney Thomas M. Gunter, merchant James H. Stirman, and attorney David Walker, all of Fayetteville, and John P.A. Parks. The secessionist candidates were Charles W. Deane, John Billingsley, and W.T. Neal.

On February 18, 1861, the very day that Jefferson Davis was sworn in as President of the newly formed Confederate States of America, the people of Arkansas voted on two issues. Should a state secession convention be held to consider joining the Confederacy? The voters of Washington County said no, but Arkansas as a whole said yes. Should Arkansas secede? A compilation of votes for pro-secession and pro-union candidates for delegates to the secession convention showed that the state was not ready to leave the Union.

Arkansas as a whole was strongly in favor of a secession convention, though not in favor of secession itself. The voters in Washington

Secession Convention Vote February 18, 1861			
Hold a Secession Convention?		**Should Arkansas Secede?**	
Yes	No	Yes	No
Washington County:			
569 27%	1,541 73%	410 18%	1,924 82%
Arkansas Total:			
27,412 63%	15,826 37%	17,927 43%	23,626 57%

County very strongly neither wanted secession nor a secession convention. Nonetheless, a convention was to be held, and as delegates Washington County selected the unionist candidates. The votes were Stirman 1,924, Gunter, 1,780, Parks 1,763, and Walker, 1,777. Those not winning were the secessionists Deane, 410 votes, Billingsley 364, Neal 353, and scattering 42.[55]

The Arkansian reported that "[t]he election on Monday passed off, under all circumstances, as quietly as our elections generally do, without bloodshed or angry feeling, and the Union is doing as well as could be expected."[56] David Walker was exuberant, writing in a letter on the 18th that "The national flag waves above us. The enthusiasm is great. The vote...we suppose is ten to one for the Union ticket. Our success is certain."[57] The people of Fayetteville and the state looked forward with anxiety to the secession convention to be held in a little more than two weeks.

On March 4th Abraham Lincoln was inaugurated President of the United States. The upper South, including Arkansas, waited anxiously to know what he said, and the words of his inaugural address in Washington, D.C., were wired to both Fayetteville and to the state convention in Little Rock.

Lincoln made six main points. First, he would take no direct action against slavery where it already existed. "I have no purpose, directly or indirectly, to interfere with the institution of slavery in the States where it exists. I believe I have no lawful right to do so, and I have no inclination to do so.... Second, the Union was perpetual and could not be dissolved. "I hold that in contemplation of universal law and of the Constitution the Union of these States is perpetual. Perpetuity is implied, if not expressed, in the fundamental law of all national governments. It is safe to assert that no government proper ever had a provision in its organic law for its own termination."

Third, Lincoln explained that he would maintain the government. "I therefore consider that in view of the Constitution and the laws the Union is unbroken, and to the extent of my ability, I shall take care, as the Constitution itself expressly enjoins upon me, that the laws of the Union be faithfully executed in *all* the States." Fifth, he would maintain Ft. Sumter in Charleston harbor and all federal properties. "[T]he Union...*will* constitutionally defend and maintain itself.... The power confided to me will be used to hold, occupy, and possess the property and places belonging to the Government and to collect the duties and imposts." Fifth, President Lincoln said that he would start no war. "[T]here needs to be no bloodshed or violence, and there shall be none unless it be forced upon the national authority."

Lastly, Lincoln called for Southerners to carefully consider their course: "That there are persons in one section or another who seek to destroy the Union at all events and are glad of any pretext to do it I will neither affirm nor deny; but if there be such, I need address no word to them. To those, however, who really love the Union may I not speak?

"Before entering upon so grave a matter as the destruction of our national fabric, with all its benefits, its memories, and its hopes, would it not be wise to ascertain precisely why we do it? Will you hazard so desperate a step while there is any possibility that any portion of the ills you fly from have no real existence? Will you, while the certain ills you fly to are greater than all the real ones you fly from, will you risk the commission of so fearful a mistake?...

"My countrymen, one and all, think calmly and *well* upon this whole subject. Nothing valuable can be lost by taking time.... In *your* hands, my dissatisfied fellow-countrymen, and not in *mine,* is the momentous issue of civil war.... I am loath to close. We are not enemies, but friends. We must not be enemies. Though passion may have strained it must not break our bonds of affection. The mystic chords of memory, stretching from every battlefield and patriot grave to every living heart and hearthstone all over this broad land, will yet swell the chorus of the Union, when again touched, as surely they will be, by the better angels of our nature."[58]

In general, the people of Fayetteville, the state of Arkansas and the South as a region did not like the speech. Why did they reject Lincoln's plea? In the final analysis, it was because the two sections of the United States had developed different visions of America. Lincoln articulated the Northern vision, but there was a Southern vision as well, and the two in 1861 were no longer compatible. Minds were already made up; opinions were set beyond the point where further discussion had any chance of persuasion. It was as true of the North as it was of the South.

The Southern view was presented by President Jefferson Davis of the Confederate States of America in his inaugural address as President in Montgomery, Alabama. On February 18th, fifteen days before Lincoln spoke, Davis raised his hand and was sworn into office. He explained that the Union was not perpetual, but created by states that were originally sovereign, and were still sovereign, capable of withdrawing from the compact they had formed at the time of the Revolution. The United States was founded upon the principle of government by consent of the governed, and when the governed withdrew their consent, they could form a new nation of their own choosing. The Southern states were now withdrawing their consent.

This new Confederacy was "[a]ctuated solely by the desire to preserve our own rights and promote our own welfare," and its creation "has been marked by no aggression upon others and followed by no domestic convulsion." It was foreseeable to Davis that other Southern states would eventually join the Confederacy. "[I]t is not unreasonable to expect that States from which we have recently parted may seek to unite their fortunes with ours under the Government which we have instituted," he said, surely thinking that Arkansas was in this group.

The "rights" that were to be preserved included the political principle of states' rights. Although the words "slave" and "slavery" did not appear in Davis's address, everyone knew that another right to be preserved was the right of white people to own slaves. There were other interests to be protected, such as Southern nationalism, freedom from the control of the Northern majority, and preservation of an agricultural society against growing Northern industrialism. The differences with the Northern states were substantial and real, and Southerners no longer wished to remain in the association with them.

Davis mentioned in his address that though other Southern states may want to unite with the Confederacy under its new constitution, "a reunion with the States from which we have separated is neither practicable nor desirable."[59]

It was within this political setting that President Lincoln's inaugural address was wired in full from Washington, D.C., to both Little Rock and Fayetteville. For such an important document to be so quickly transmitted to the edge of American settlements was unprecedented, and wouold not have been possible just a year earlier.

On the same day that Lincoln was being inaugurated, the Arkansas secession convention was called to order in Little Rock. David Walker of Fayetteville was elected chairman, and Elias C. Boudinot, who moved away from Fayetteville the year before to edit a newspaper in Van Buren, was appointed secretary. It was a sure sign that the unionists were in control.

The next day in Fayetteville a meeting at the courthouse in Fayetteville appointed a committee that drew up a resolution that "the inhabitants of Arkansas being inseparably connected with the Southern States, she should immediately take such steps as would guarantee her safety," whatever that meant. The committee drawing up the resolutions consisted of Dr. Samuel R. Bell, Charles W. Deane, J.P. Doss, James D. Walker and Robert Buchanan, representing people from across Washington County. The resolution adopted stated:

> Whereas, the inaugural address of Mr. Lincoln clearly indicates his intention to retake the forts and arsenals of the seceded States, and, also, to collect the revenue in said States, and
> Whereas, Virginia, Kentucky and other border States have declared that such an attempt would be coercion. Therefore, be it
> Resolved, that in our opinion, the inhabitants of Arkansas being inseparably connected with the Southern States, she should immediately take such steps as would guarantee her safety.[60]

The Arkansas delegates on March 5th took a preliminary vote, rejecting secession 35 to 40. The vote revealed a class and geographic split between northwest farmers and southeast planters. Two representatives from South Carolina addressed the convention, but could not persuade any change. After two weeks of speeches, the final vote came on March 16th. Secession lost 35 to 39. The convention adjourned, subject to being recalled by Chairman David Walker should circumstances warrant further consideration.

For the next four weeks people waited anxiously to see what would happen. Would the North let the South go in peace or would there be war? Rumors circulated about whether Union troops would hold Fort Sumter, whether Lincoln would reinforce it, and whether Confederates would attack it.

Even if there was a war, what did the people of Fayetteville have to fear? Arkansas was the least populous of any state that may join the Confederacy, and the least important. The town itself was in a remote corner of that state, a thousand miles from the likely battles to occur in Virginia. Yes, local young men may have to go far away to war, but it would have seemed the remotest possibility, or an impossibility, that war would come to Fayetteville. The war would probably be short, anyway, many believed, with the Northerners giving up after a military defeat or two. Doubtless both secessionists and unionists in Fayetteville would have been disheartened to know how unimportant Abraham Lincoln and Jefferson Davis thought Arkansas was in the overall scheme of things.

"[W]e saw nothing to indicate that *our* region would be made the seat of war," wrote Pastor Baxter. "Secure amid our mountains, we thought that the faint murmurs of strife would reach us from the seaboard and the great rivers, where alone, we thought, it would rage, for our distance from great streams and railways and our comparatively thin settlements were unfavorable to the march and subsistence of a large army." That assumption, though logical when made, would prove to be vastly in error.

Everyday life went on, though distracted by national events. In March William A. Watson succeeded Elias Moore as Fayetteville's postmaster. On March 2, 1861, Congress passed a law terminating the Butterfield run into Confederate territory effective July 1, 1861. It would have stopped about that time anyway, as it went right through the future battlefield of Wilson's Creek.

On December 12, 1860, the bachelor merchant Joseph Holcomb married 21-year-old Cener Boone, a niece of Dr. James Boone and a cousin of Lafayette Boone and Benjamin F. Boone. On April 3,

1861, Fayetteville attorney James R. Pettigrew, 29, married 18-year-old Alvira Reagan, the daughter of his senior law partner, Wilburn Reagan.[61] It was probably the last big social wedding in town before the killing started.

Fayetteville secessionists were not waiting around for politicians to make a formal declaration. A Rebel flag was raised on the pole in the courthouse yard in Fayetteville on April 6, before the shooting had begun and before Arkansas had seceded from the Union. Sarah Dickson, 38, the wife of town merchant Joseph L. Dickson, made a speech and presented the flag to Dr. Charles W. Deane. *The Arkansasian* reported on April 12th that "the beautiful banner floated out gallantly to the breeze. The Brass Band then struck up 'Dixie's Land'* after which three cheers were proposed for Jeff Davis and the Southern Confederacy, which was responded to by the immense throng with a hearty good will."

Wilburn Reagan, standing beneath the secessionist banner, made a strong appeal for leaving the Union. Thomas Gunter was called out to oppose him, and he accepted the challenge, but, pointing to the flag, refused to speak under the "damnable rag." He called for the meeting to adjourn to the courthouse. Tempers were flaring as the people went into the courthouse. Thomas Wilhite, a strong unionist from Fall Creek, twenty miles south of Fayetteville, and about twenty other armed men, protected Gunter as he spoke. The attorney called for the Union to be preserved and said he would vote against secession.[62] *The Arkansian* account of the incident closed with this comment: "We cannot conclude this article and deny the need of praise that is due the saloon keepers who at the request of the ladies, closed their doors during the day."

The same day that the flag went up the flagpole in Fayetteville town square, the Confederates bombarded Fort Sumter in Charleston, South Carolina. President Lincoln sent out a call for states to contribute 75,000 men to put down the rebellion, including 780 from Arkansas. The suspense was over. There would be war.

---

* The song Dixie was written by Dan Emmett for a New York City Broadway minstrel band in September 1859. It was played as a marching tune for Southern patriotism for the first time at the inauguration of Jefferson Davis as President of the Confederacy on February 18, 1861. The song swept the South and became its unofficial anthem. Thirty years before, when Emmett was fifteen years old, he had written another popular tune, "Old Dan Tucker."

Arkansas Governor Henry M. Rector, along with all Southern governors, refused to support Lincoln's call for troops. Instead, Southern nationalism and war fever swept the state. Many who had opposed secession were even more opposed to fighting against other Southern states, and if required to choose between these two alternatives, would and did choose secession. On April 27th a call went out from David Walker for the secession convention to reconvene. By the time the delegates reassembled in Little Rock on May 6th, Virginia had already seceded and Tennessee was meeting for the same purpose.

After the fighting at Fort Sumter and before the Arkansas secession convention again convened, Judge David Walker in April issued an address "to the people of Washington County." He asked what the people would have him do under these new circumstances of war. "What will you have your delegates do?" he asked. He gave alternative courses of action as remaining in the Union, seceding to remain independent as a single state, or seceding to join the Confederacy. "There never was a time when we should act with more prudence than at present.... I desire to know your will."[63] The will expressed to him was apparently for secession, for when he arrived in Little Rock to chair the convention, he voted to leave the Union.

"An Ordinance to dissolve the union now existing between the State of Arkansas and the other States united with her under the compact entitled, 'The Constitution of the United States of America'" was introduced to the convention. The Unionists were in disarray and under tremendous popular pressure. Like Walker, most Unionists had changed their minds; others could not withstand the tidal wave. The convention voted 64 to 5 to secede. Of the Washington County delegates, only Thomas Gunter was still voting against secession. As chairman Walker called for the five to change their votes to make it unanimous, and all did except one of the northwest delegates, Isaac Murphy of Huntsville. The final tally is 60 to 1. At ten minutes past four on the afternoon of May 6, 1861, Arkansas became the tenth state to leave the Union.

Back in Fayetteville, the excitement was intense. Confederate patriotism was at its peak. But not all were glad. Upon hearing of Arkansas' secession a sorrowful Jonas Tebbetts took an eagle he had been keeping and let it go as a gesture of freedom. Tebbetts was truly torn by the conflicting loyalties of North and South. An interesting description of Tebbetts was given by Homer Tebbetts Gailey, his grandson. "If Judge Tebbetts had any lingering affection for the North, it was the South he loved. He had married a Southern girl...who had inherited slaves. He himself had adopted the Southern way of life and lived within those traditions. He had a deep sympathy for the people of the South and unlike most Northerners, he understood their economic and social problems and their political philosophy. But he could not bear the thought of secession. He loved the Union more than any of its component parts."[64]

Amid talk of war and volunteering for soldiering, one of the final acts of peace was the graduation at the Fayetteville Female Seminary. Among other young women, Lizzie J. Van Hoose received her certificate. "Miss Lizzie J. Van Hoose has completed the prescribed course of study at the Fayetteville Female Seminary and by her attainments and correct deportment is entitled to this Testimonial." It was signed by Lucretia Foster Smith, the principal. Another student graduating that spring was young Mary Stone. and by her attainments and correct deportment is entitled to this Testimonial." .

Lizzie Van Hoose. Van Hoose Family Papers, (MC 583), Special Collections, University of Arkansas Libraries, Fayetteville.

Another student graduating that spring was young Mary Stone. and by her attainments and correct deportment is entitled to this Testimonial." There would never be another graduation. Lucretia Smith would never teach again as she would not survive the coming strife.

The Call to Arms

Events were running faster than the formalities of conventions and politicians. In Fayetteville Dr. Samuel R. Bell, a 37-year-old born in Tennessee, declared for the Confederacy and was raising a company of volunteers to join in the war, called the Pike Guards after a former resident of town, Albert Pike. On May 2nd the enlistment was held, even while Arkansas was still in the Union. One came imagine the excitement and hubbub of the townspeople as young men gathered. Who would join? Where would they go? What would happen to them? Young men were anxious or reluctant, perhaps encouraged or discouraged by heartfelt conversations with parents or wives.

Regimental records for each unit name the volunteers stepped forward. M.C. Duke, who had been accused of being a secessionist at the town meeting three months earlier, confirmed the allegation by enlisting and was made First Sergeant of this first company of Confederates. The newspaper editor Elias B. Moore was made Second Sergeant. It must have been with a feeling of trepidation that the widow Christiana Watson saw her 25-year-old son Frank go as Third Sergeant and 18-year-old son Joseph enlist as a private. Martin L Hawkins, still a teenager and the clerk at the courthouse, joined. His mother, Jane, was also a widow. His father, a Kentucky veteran of the War of 1812, had died about the time Martin was born. Jane's feelings can easily be imagined.

William H. Brooks, a Michigan native turned Confederate, leading 34th Arkansas Infantry. His brother, Edwards Brooks, became the Colonel of a Union regiment of Arkansas soldiers. Prairie Grove Battlefield State Park.

State Representative Benjamin F. Boone put his name on the line. George House, a 20-year-old blacksmith, joined. Thomas Jefferson Pollard, Jr., merchant and son of the doctor, volunteered as a private, along with his brother John. So did Jack McRoy, 22-year-old Erastus Stirman, and William Smith (son of the printer). The painter Nicholas Wax joined, as did the dentist John R. Palmer. Others from Washington County, including Marshall Henry, who lived just two miles north of town, and James W. Stirman, son of J. Harvey Stirman, also joined in Captain Bell's company. William H. Brooks, a promising young attorney just a year in the area from his home in Michigan, was a Confederate all the way. This company contained a good deal of the young manhood of Fayetteville, all enlisted by their own act before Arkansas had even left the Union.

It was during this time of recruitment that Dr./Captain Bell and Pastor Baxter bumped into each other at the telegraph office. The two fell into a short debate that neither could win. Bell said the North had forced the war; Baxter said the South had started it by firing the first shot at Sumter. The minister said that one could not expect the North to submit after such an event. "On this he flamed out on language most bitter and threatening," recorded Baxter, "intimating that such sentiments would no longer be tolerated."[65] Baxter failed to mention that in the North secession sentiments were no longer tolerated, and dissenters were jailed without right of habeas corpus. Civil war is not a debate; it happens when people are killing mad.

Before leaving his duties as an editor, young Elias Moore explained himself in his newspaper. "We have felt it our duty to drop the pen and composing stick and to leave home, friends and all that is near and dear to us," he wrote romantically but honestly in *The Fayetteville Democrat*, "and shoulder our rifle and march forward to defend our common country against an invading enemy."[66] The invasion argument was a true one. The South did not invade the North; it was the North that sent troops into the South.

Pastor Baxter saw his college disintegrate, first into philosophical debating factions, then into angry divisions, and finally into fighting soldiers. When "recruiting and volunteering began," he wrote, "the feeling among the students on both sides grew warmer; those who were in favor of enlisting began to accuse those who were loyally disposed with a want of courage; the pressure of public sentiment in favor of all young men going into the army began to have its influence, till at length, early in May, a young man, who had ever advocated the Union side, stung, doubtless, by the taunts of cowardice which now began to be heard, closed an address to the students assembled in the college hall for religious and literary exercises, with the words, "Let us die like men!" He was cheered tumultuously, the resolve was taken, the die was cast; they gathered around me, and spoke of the necessity which was upon them, and of their determination to enlist. I bade them meet me yet once more on the next morning; and feeling that parting was inevitable, with tears which were answered by their tears, I uttered my farewell."

The women of Fayetteville were doing what they could for the cause, making flags and uniforms and encouraging their men to join the military. It was reported that the Pike Guards had the first stars and bars flag in the state. Martha Pollard, the 22-year-old wife of Thomas Pollard and daughter-in-law of the doctor, was given the honor of delivering a farewell speech to the Pike Guards on May 2nd when the flag was presented to them:

> "This is indeed an uncommon occasion that has called us together today - a novel scene in our quiet little village.
>
> "Drum and fife awaken strange echoes from our peaceful mountain sides. Wonderful scenes are being enacted around us. Events are now transpiring that in years past were predicted by far-seeing men, and brought still nearer home to us by being talked of around our firesides.
>
> "Alas they are no longer to be looked forward to and dreaded as things in the future, for they are with us and around us. Truly we are in the midst of war, and with all it has come upon us while we yet slumbered; but the trumpet peal of war has sounded from side to side of our country and her brave sons have given a ready and noble response to the call; they come leaving the plowshare in the furrow, the axe beside the tree and the hammer upon the anvil; they come to join in this terrible struggle for their rights.
>
> "This will be a war such as the pages of history have never before been called upon to chronicle, one in which brother will meet brother, a father meet son and friend meet friend.
>
> "Rebellion and treason will be linked with your name; but when has independence sought to wrest her rights from the hand of tyranny that it has not been called treason? Was not Washington, who rose as the voice of an outraged people, called a traitor and a rebel?...
>
> "There is, perhaps, not one in this vast assemblage that has not dropped a tear or treasured away in some secret recess of their heart a regret for the downfall of such a government as ours has been, the crumbling to pieces of the greatest republic the world has ever known. But it has been severed, not by one mighty blow, but by the faithful labor of years. It has been chiseled apart, stroke by stroke, as drop by drop water wears a mighty stone.
>
> "The downfall has been, the dissolution now is, and we have established ourselves free and independent - mighty we will be, and respected by the world. May the little flag first raised by woman's hands upon Southern soil, fanned by Southern breezes, spread itself from side to side until it waves its bright folds at once in the blue waters of the Atlantic and the Pacific.
>
> "Now the contest has come and we must meet it. Women must meet the trial of giving up fathers and brothers, husbands and sons, and

you must meet it as men to go bear all the hardships and endure, if need be, all the terrors of war, unflinchingly....

"We have fashioned for you this flag to bear with you through the scenes of bloodshed and devastation, pain and woe. Mid the terror and heartsickness attendant upon them, remember your homes; remember you have kind friends, and friends whose hearts beat strong and high for you, who await you with warm welcome, who upon bended knee beseech the God infinite to extend his protecting arm over you, to guard and guide you safely through, and may you never forget through all that the all seeing eye is open upon you and that the hand that metes out alike reward and punishment is extended over you.

"I now present to you this flag - feeling that with it, it is unnecessary for me to urge you on to valorous deeds - to bid you bring it back to be treasured as one of the relics of Fayetteville, to bring it back, though stained with blood - crowned with glory.

"Too well I know that you, sons of the South, sons of a clime where white men are not serfs, have hearts filled with brave and noble sentiments - have wills strong enough for the emergency you go to meet.

"You go from us today buoyed by a determination, an innate power of endurance that knows no conquering.

"You go to fight for victory or death!"[67]

Following Mrs. Pollards oration, the Pike Guards marched off under Captain Bell. Then a new round of enlistments occurred in June. Americus V. Rieff, a 31-year-old Fayetteville resident with a wife and two young children, organized a company of cavalry. Rieff himself was a carpenter. So was John Brandenburg, another enlistee, who had been married only a year and left his 18-year-old bride for the adventures of war. The two oldest sons of Thomas (another carpenter) and Martha Williford, also joined. Nelson Williford, 20, as Fourth Corporal somehow outranked his 21-year-old old brother, Henry.

Others also signed up. Attorney Elias C. Boudinot returned to Fayetteville and enlisted as a private. James R. Pettigrew, a 31-year-old attorney and married just two months, bade his teenaged bride farewell. Isaac Taylor left Byrnside's Hotel to be a First Lieutenant. Andrew McGarrah, of the extended McGarrah clan, and Augustus Lewis, 25-year-old son of farmers Joseph and Mary Lewis, joined, as did many from the nearby countryside.

Thomas J. Kelly raised another company in Fayetteville, which included some of the town men. Attorney Lafayette Boone was his first lieutenant. John Parks and James Moore were second and third sergeants. John Crawford, John Frazer, John Pollard, and James Pollard enlisted as privates. This company was placed if the Fifth Arkansas State Troops.

Other Fayetteville men joined other units. Fayetteville attorney James D. Walker, 30, became the Colonel commanding the Fourth Arkansas State Troops. One of his companies had fellow attorney Thomas M. Gunter as a captain and brother-in-law Wythe Walker as a first lieutenant. Yet another attorney, Lafayette Boone, was a first lieutenant in the Fifth Arkansas State Troops. The new units organized and marched away, and much of the youth of the town was gone.

It was an exciting day in Fayetteville when the first Confederate soldiers arrived in town. Pastor Baxter described the Pelican Rifles from southern Arkansas when they marched in. "Most of them were fine-looking fellows, some of them men of wealth, position, and influence; some of them in former years students of Arkansas College. Their march had been a long one, their drill was perfect, their step and look that of veterans, their arms and uniform all that could be desired; their number, though small, seemed large to people unaccustomed to military spectacles; and when with drums beating and banners flying they marched into the College grounds, and their tents rose as by magic through that hitherto peaceful inclosure, the enthusiasm of the people knew no bounds. A most liberal hospitality was manifested by the citizens; the ladies serenaded their defenders, and the soldiers in gallant style responded with 'Advance the Flag of Dixie!'"

The excitement about a new nation, the new soldiers, the mixed emotions of war, all must have put an air of frenzy into Fayetteville. The 3rd Louisiana Infantry came in. Hundreds of men were in the area, wearing strange uniforms. Military couriers rode in and out. Supplies were being purchased everywhere. There was talk of a battle sure to take place soon in Missouri.

The confidence of the new Southern soldiers was boundless. Baxter remarked that "[n]early all the young men were perfectly familiar with the use of fire-arms.... Such was the contempt for the unwarlike North, that secession orators did not scruple to say that not a thimble-full of blood need be shed in order to secure the independence of the South...." The greatest fault of Baxter's writing was its failure to acknowledge that the feelings, actions and wrongs that he observed in the South were also prevalent in the North, though in the reverse direction. "The ladies, too," he observed, "caught the war spirit; uniforms, sashes, and banners grew under their active hands."

The Northern-born people of Fayetteville were by now wondering what to do. Should they leave at once or stay to see what happened?. Probably one of the first to leave was Charlie Butterfield, who likely returned to New York as soon as the stage route was stopped by Congress in March. Thomas Van Horne went North in 1861, presumably after school dismissed in early summer. Some Northerners who appeared in the census simply are not mentioned again, so they likely left town.

On July 4, 1861, Jonas Tebbetts gathered his family quietly in their home. He read to them the Declaration of Independence and revealed a secretly held flag of the United States. He decided to stay on, as did William Baxter and others.

The War Begins for Fayetteville

After the shooting at Fort Sumter in April, it took many weeks for both sides to assemble their armies. The Pike Guards marched northward into Missouri. On July 1st Private Ras Stirman sent a letter to his teenage sister, Rebecca, back in Fayetteville. "I think I will make a tolerable good soldier," he said, which certainly became true as he soon rose to the rank of colonel as a very young man. "I think there will be a chance for a fight Shortly," he also accurately predicted. In the bravado of untried youth he boasted, "Telling you about the anticipated fight with the duch [Dutch] need not frighten you out of your witts for me," he wrote in reference to the German soldiers in the Union Army, "for the duch can't hit me."[68]

Although preparing for war and despite the occurrence of a few minor skirmishes, the South by default enjoyed a half year of peace and undisputed Confederate sovereignty in 1861. A permanent Southern independence seemed to be very close with the great eastern victory in Virginia on July 21, 1861, in a battle called Manassas in the Confederacy and Bull Run in the North.

The news of the tidings of that battle was received with joy or disappointment, depending upon one's politics. "The first battle of

Bull Run was fought with such a result as convinced all Southern men of the propriety of the estimate they had placed on Northern valor," Baxter wrote. "Union men...were startled at the news and depressed by the general exultation."

The Southern army moved into Missouri and it was know that a significant battle would be fought soon. In a letter of August 6th, before any battle occurred, David Walker's wife Mary wrote to her husband who was at the front. The letter illustrates the stress that she and countless other women were under. "You can easily imagine my uneasiness since the first news of an engagement reached us. A thousand dreadful thoughts have been mine day and night," she wrote, "and if I had not naturally been of a sanguine temperament I should not have been able to have born the suspense. But thank God you are yet spared and I will trust His Goodness and Mercy to bring you safely back to me... I don't feel like writing. I would tell you everything if I could only see you but I am so nervous and anxious that I can't think of the news if there is any and I don't feel like writing it anyway... Oh, may the God of battles preserve my dear, dear David is the prayer of his devoted and anxious Mary."[69]

The eastern Confederate victory at Manassas was followed up three weeks later on August 10th with a great western victory near Springfield, Missouri, just a hundred miles from Fayetteville. It would not be unreasonable to say that after these two battles the Confederacy was at its zenith. This battle was known as Oak Hills in the South and Wilson's Creek in the North. When news of the Confederate victory reached Fayetteville, the gladness with which it was received among secessionists is not difficult to imagine.

It would not have been long, however, until the cost of victory reached home. For the first time, the war touched Fayetteville with a heavy hand. The Pike Guards, with a good share of the cream of Fayetteville's youth, had been in the thick of the fighting. Gladness for victory surely gave way to shock and disbelief. Samuel R. Bell, the company commander and longtime local doctor known to all, was dead, shot through the left breast. Another doctor's son, Thomas Pollard, known as Jeff, was wounded in the right arm. Second Sergeant Elias B. Moore was shot through the right thigh with a musket ball. Martin L. Hawkins, the 19-year-old assistant to County Clerk and youngest child of Fayetteville's widowed Jane Hawkins, was dead on the field with a minie ball through the center of the forehead. Nick Wax was slightly wounded in the shoulder. Marshall Henry was badly but not mortally wounded. In all, the Pike Guards lost four killed and eight wounded.[70] This was not a great number, but coming from a single town, in was devastating to a people unused to war.

Fayetteville's soldiers had given a good account of themselves, but also paid the price demanded by the gods of war. Ras Stirman of the Pike Guards hastily penned a letter to his sister the very day of the battle. "Thank God I am preserved," he said. "Sis it was a desperate affare.... They opened up on us bringing us down like Sheep but we never wave[re]d. We did not wait for orders to fire but all of us cut loose at them like wild men, then we dropt to our nees and loded and Shot as fast as we could, we had to shoot by guess as they were upon the hill lying in the grass.... I think providence interferred in my behalf.... McCulloch has complimented us Saying our regiment Saved the day. It was warm times I tell you."[71] Stirman wrote out the names of the company's casualties and the nature of their wounds.

This was real war. A good deal of Fayetteville's enthusiasm and romanticism likely evaporated that day, replaced in some people with a realistic determination, and in others with a heartsick disillusionment. David Walker was present at the battle and two days later sent a letter to his wife, Mary. "Oh it was a sickening sight to pass over the battle field and see the dead lying in every direction," he wrote.

The anxiety of the families of the soldiers was reflected in a letter written by David Walker's daughter, Mary. "I have been very uneasy about you all since the news of the battle first reached us," she wrote on August 16th. "So many different reports are given concerning it that it is impossible to learn the truth. Twas a dearly bought victory to us, and has caused many an affectionate heart to groan with anguish. Poor Aunt Jane [Hawkins] is inconsolable. Upon hearing of Martin's death I went to see her, and found her almost heartbroken."[72]

As soon as word of the battle reached Fayetteville, Presley Smith, Alfred M. Wilson and Dr. Charles W. Deane immediately departed for the site in Missouri to gather details of what had happened. The soldiers of Oak Hills/Wilson's Creek came streaming home within just a few days. The Arkansas state troops were disbanded. Americus Rieff's company, which served in the battle as scouts and escorts independently of any regiment and reported directly to General Ben McCulloch, was discharged in Springfield just three days after the fighting. They had suffered no casualties. On September 1st the Pike Guards were released, going home to tell their stories of bravery and horror.

The war, of course, was not over. The Northern troops did not, after all, go home after a couple of good lickings at Manassas and Oak Hills. The discharged Arkansas state troops were now re-recruited for service in the Confederate army. The buzz of military rallying and enlisting began all over again. This time, though, it was with a greater feeling of reality. Many of those who had gone before were not so inclined to leave again on another military adventure.

Through the last months of 1861 Colonel William H. Brooks of Fayetteville was busy raising several companies of men in several Arkansas counties. On October 9th Captain Matthew O. Davidson was in Fayetteville, signing up another company of cavalry. Twenty-one-year-old Perry Davidson, the son of merchant Elija and Nancy, was designated as the company's chief musician. William O. Feemster, son of the South Carolina-born Presbyterian minister, became a sergeant. So did carpenter John Frazer. The Smith and Williford families stepped forward. James Smith, John Smith and William Smith, who were apparently two brothers and a cousin but all of Fayetteville, enlisted for the first time. Henry and Nelson Williford, who had been in Rieff's company and seen no action, signed up again, this time with both as privates. Steele Stanford and Albert O. McCollum, who lived just outside of town, enlisted as privates. This company was later designated as Company E of Ras Stirman's Cavalry Battalion.

Before the month was out, on October 26th, Captain Lafayette Boone, an attorney of Fayetteville, was enlisting yet another company. Some of the former Pike Guards signed up for this unit. John Pollard was back, but without his wounded brother, Thomas. Private John Brandenburg, formerly of Rieff's Company, again volunteered. James C. Parks, brother of Elizabeth Jane Blakeley, was a private. John Smith enlisted. This unit was later designated as Company D of Stirman's Cavalry.

Other Fayetteville men served the Confederacy in other ways. Dr. Thomas Jefferson Pollard, Sr., offered his medical services on an as needed basis. He had been at Oak Hills/Wilson's Creek where his son was wounded, and would serve in many other battles.[73] Bill "Cush" Quesenberry, a newspaperman in his peacetime life, joined with General Albert Pike, serving as a Quartermaster in a Confederate

Cherokee brigade from the Indian Nations. Attorney Alfred M. Wilson stayed home and became a colonel of a local militia organization.

Merchant Joseph Holcomb became a quartermaster, procuring food and other goods for General Thomas C. Hindman's army, then for the Confederate hospital at Cane Hill, and still later for the 2nd Arkansas Cavalry.[74] Attorney David Walker, too old for military service in the field, served on the military court of General Sterling Price. George Van Hoose, brother of James and Peter, became a captain in the 17th Arkansas Infantry in Ras Stirman's regiment, and took into the field with him his slave, Bob, which was commonly done among the officers. His brother Bud Van Hoose also joined a Confederate unit.[75] Elias Boudinot became the Cherokee representative in the Confederate Congress. William R. Quarles served in Company E of the 7th Arkansas Confederate Cavalry under Colonel Thomas M Gunter. Gunter estimated that about two thousand Washington County men were in the Confederate service during the war.[76]

During the remainder of 1861 there were no further major battles in northwest Arkansas or southwest Missouri. Fayetteville and all of Arkansas spent the entire year within Confederate sovereignty. The year had brought many changes. Most of the young men were gone to the war. Soldiers were coming and going. There was news of war, ceaseless rumors and an uncertain future.

Yet the town was intact, the people were still in their homes. Things would change very soon.

1862
Destruction and Death

"Fayetteville presented a sad spectacle of destruction and waste and ruin."

The Confederate government established in Montgomery, Alabama, in February of 1861 was only provisional. Once the new nation had been established, the constitution approved, and new states admitted, a permanent government was inaugurated. A general election was held in the Confederacy in November, 1861, and Jefferson Davis was elected unopposed as president for the next six years. No information about the conduct or voting of that election in Fayetteville is known. The first Congress of the Confederate States under the constitution met at Richmond, Virginia, on February 18, 1862, exactly one year from the date of Davis's provisional inauguration.

That very day, February 18th, was the last day that Fayetteville would stand in its pre-war splendor. The charming, quiet mountain town of with its schools, churches, businesses, town square, and fine homes, would be destroyed on the first full day of the permanent Confederate government.

For five months after its defeat at Wilson's Creek near Springfield, Missouri, the Union Army rebuilt its strength, and in early February 1862 it moved into northwest Arkansas. The outnumbered Confederate forces withdrew ahead of it, deciding that the time to oppose this invasion would come later. Anxiety was running high for everyone, military and civilian alike. What would happen when the blue soldiers came into this Rebel town? Should family members of Confederate soldiers stay in their homes or flee?

General Benjamin McCulloch of Texas was in command of the Rebel forces in the area. He was a hard man, disliked by Confederate civilians and hated by Unionist Southerners. As he pulled his men out of the area he decided that the abundant army supplies that had been accumulated in Fayetteville were too burdensome to be moved. But neither could they, he felt, be simply be left to the Federals. He permitted his men to take away from the supplies in town whatever foodstuffs they could carry.

The retreating soldiers started taking the goods of Fayetteville with vigor. They were demoralized by the flight in the face of the enemy. The marching was disorganized and the officers had little control of the men, and the entire effect was most un-military. Many civilians were fleeing, too, going south and taking with them their animals and slaves to prevent their liberation by the approaching Federals. This civilian flight surely included Fayetteville residents, as few slaves were left in town to be liberated .

First the soldiers took only the army supplies that were permitted. Then the taking spread to businesses and homes. A general looting began, soon widening into a free-for-all pillage of much of Fayetteville. Stores and private homes were ransacked.

Reverend William Baxter recorded the event:

[S]o general had the work of destruction and plunder become, that it was almost impossible to find a single soldier who did not possess some evidence of being carried away by the spirit of the hour. Here was one with a cigar box half filled with sugar, another with a pair of lady's gaiters sticking out of his pocket; this had a pair of baby's shoes, that, some fine lace; artificial flowers adorned the caps of some; while jars of pickles, tin cups full of molasses, tape, calico, school-books, letters, law papers, sheets of tin plate, in fact nearly every article known to traffic might have been seen in that motley throng. Indeed, any one could see at a glance that the greater part of them had taken articles for which they had no use whatever. Some contented themselves with what really belonged to them - the army stores; and many a wagon filled with fine quarters of beef was hastily unloaded in the street, to be replaced by bacon, immense piles of which had been collected for the use of the various camps in the vicinity.

Whole companies would march out of town, each man with a ham, shoulder, or side of bacon on his bayonet, and no one could complain of them for thus wishing to change their camp fare.... Officers threatened, cursed, called them thieves, made appeals to their manliness and State pride, and to the fact that they were among those battling in the same cause; but all in vain; stealing had become a kind of recreation, and they would steal. Gen. Price himself strove to check the disorder which I have attempted faintly to describe, but for once his commands were powerless, and the work of ruin went on.

The scene was described by Confederate Lieutenant George Taylor of the 17th Arkansas Infantry. "Fayetteville presented indeed a sad spectacle when we passed through on the 20th," he stated. "I could not but contrast the beautiful quiet little town of last May when we were so heartily welcomed to the then devastation and waste and ruin manifest all around. Heaven help a country where an army must linger, be it friend or foe. What citizens now left in Fayetteville seemed perfectly panic-stricken.... Stores all along Main Street were thrown open to the Missouri and Arkansas soldiers. Amid the destruction it could not but be amusing to see great heavy-bearded fellows carrying around fancy little toys - rattlers, made to amuse very small juveniles. Bonnet frames -old French flowers - nearly every man had a looking glass."[77]

General Ben McCulloch gave the order to burn Fayetteville. Shiloh Museum.

The pillaging was not the worst of it. After the infantry finally withdrew, Confederate cavalrymen were sent back to set fire to many of the public buildings. General McCulloch had determined upon a scorched-earth policy of destruction. The propriety of such a policy may be debatable among military people, but it is certainly a difficult thing for civilians to understand it when their town is burned by people who are supposed to be protecting it.

The disaster was recorded by Baxter: "The next morning dawned, and in haste the officers of the retreating [Confederate] army departed. But soon bands of Cavalry...dashed into town and began firing the buildings which had been used for military purposes; some of them contained large quantities of beef and bacon, which soon added violence to the flames. Then the large stables, once the property of the Overland Mail Company, were destroyed; the steam mill, which had been furnishing the rebel army ten thousand pounds of flour per day, was consumed; and, as we gazed on the clouds of smoke pierced here and there by tongues of flame, we felt that the fate of our beautiful mountain city was sealed." The printing equipment of *The Fayetteville Democrat* was destroyed.

"The town was set on fire in a dozen different places," recalled Marian Tebbetts. "The Overland Stables made a wonderful blaze." The burning commissary supplies of food caused "dense smoke and sickening odors that surrounded the town for days and days, as that immense stock of valuable beef and bacon smouldered and was consumed. At times the smoke was so dense that it seemed like a great black cloud over town."[78]

The townspeople tried to save whatever buildings they could. Jonas Tebbetts begged officers to permit him to remove machinery from the flour mill he and Stirman and Dickson owned, but the building was burned anyway.

Elizabeth Blakely had two soldiers come to her house with orders to burn it. She pled with them not to do it, but they said they had their orders and must follow them. They placed a burning torch under the house, which Elizabeth quickly put out. This, apparently, was what the soldiers intended. They could easily have restrained her and put the house into flames had they really wanted to do so.

Next, Elizabeth had to deal with the Masonic building nearby. "My mistress, Mrs. Blakeley...kept the Masonic Building from being burned," recalled the former slave Adeline Blakeley many years later. "The soldiers came to set it on fire. Mrs. Blakeley knew that if it burned, our home would burn as it was just across the street. Mrs. Blakeley had two small children who were very ill in upstairs rooms. She told the soldiers if they burned the masonic Building that her house would burn and she would be unable to save her little children. They went away"[79] In the war years to come, when church congregations were able to meet, they gathered at the Masonic hall saved by Elizabeth Blakely.

Reverend Baxter intervened to save the Fayetteville Female Institute of Robert Van Horne, but in vain. He described the event in detail:

About fifty yards from my residence was a large and beautiful structure, in the days of peace a Female College, but latterly used as a military arsenal and cartridge manufactory," he wrote. "The ammunition had been removed, with the exception of a large quantity of condemned bombshells - the fuses imperfect, but the shells charged with the elements of destruction. A soldier, lately one of our citizens, rode up to this building, dismounted, and just when entering was addressed by some persons living near, and informed them that he was sent to destroy it; but he evidently had little taste for the deed. The danger to the women and children in the dwellings near, from the explosion of the shells in the building, was pointed out to him, and though it involved disobedience of orders, he declared he would do no such deed, remounted and rode off.

Scarcely was he out of sight, when a few horsemen galloped up, entered the building, and began to make preparations for burning it by pouring turpentine on the floors and between the ceilings; permission was asked to remove bombshells, but they refused; the torch was applied, and the flames spread so rapidly that the occupants of the next building had scarcely time to save their trunks and some bedding, before that was also on fire.

My own house was now in great danger, and we began to remove what we deemed most valuable; but before we had succeeded to any great extent, the fire reached the bombshells; a terrific explosion took place, not less than twenty bursting at once, scattering the deadly fragments in a hundred directions. Sending away the children to a place of safety, we still strove to save some of our effects from my residence, to which the fire had now reached.

The Pastor succeeded in saving his home.

Across the street to the north, the Jonas Tebbetts family was making the same effort. "[T]he pieces of bursting shells kept everyone under roof protection except Hale and Harris," recalled daughter Marian, "who dodged from chimney to chimney with buckets of water to extinguish firebrands that fell thick and fast on the shingles." Their house was also saved.

According to Baxter "[t]he few citizens who remained could do little toward arresting the progress of fires in so many different places at the same time; and when night fell a great portion of our town was a smouldering ruin."

The day of February 22, 1862, witnessed a lull in the catastrophe. Fayetteville lay between two close armies, one a short distance to the north, another nearby to the south. The town lay largely in ruins; the people were in shock.

The same day in Richmond, Virginia, the ceremonies instituting the new government were continued. Congress had begun on the 18th. Now, on February 22, 1862, Jefferson Davis was sworn in as the President of the Confederate States of America under the new constitution. The day was chosen because it was the birthday of George Washington. In the secure Confederate capital city Davis raised his hand and was cheered by a supporting crowd. "After a series of successes and victories, which covered our arms with glory," he said honestly, "we have recently met with serious disasters." No town had a bigger disaster befall it than Fayetteville had the day before. Davis went on, saying hopefully, "But in the heart of a people resolved to be free, these disasters tend but to stimulate increased resistance."[80]

More disasters were coming for Fayetteville. "The next morning, early, [our slave] Betty came to arouse the family," wrote Marian Tebbetts. Something unusual was happening on the...northern edge of town.... All the family collected in the yard to watch. Sometimes there was flash of light as if the sun shining on metal, then a horse came into sight - a bit of blue. One had not long to wait. Down the hill, down the old Overland road, a line of blue began to form.... [A] line of battle was formed directly back of our house."

Baxter was watching the same scene from his house: "Within a few moments men had been slain and wounded, prisoners taken, and our town was in possession of the advance guard of the Union army." Confederate sovereignty had been interrupted in Fayetteville for the first time.

General Alexander Asboth commanded the Union troops who marched into town. Someone told him that the stars and stripes that had once flown over the courthouse was in the possession of the Tebbetts family. "In a short time, an officer appeared as the door and courteously requested the flag, which she willingly but with apprehension gave up," recalled Marian. It was raised over the Washington County Courthouse in town square. "[O]f those who loved it," Marian said of the flag, "some cheered and some wept."

Marian described how her home for the first time became headquarters for the army: "Gen. Asboth made his headquarters at our house, and again there were soldiers and soldiers... The great kindly Hungarian, booted to the thighs and his staff similarly booted, were everywhere in the house...getting information from Father, petting the children, trying to help Betty set the long table, sending in coffee and sugar and salt, the things most needed in our depleted larder; the General begging permission to bring York - his great Dane - to table with him, and with which he shared dainties."⁸¹

Baxter felt exhilarated. "The house of Judge Tebbetts, opposite mine, was chosen as Head-Quarters," he said, full of hope, "and we all felt glad in the thought that we should never again be left among our enemies, but that they would press on and stand between us and danger. Soon I walked down to the public square, and there saw a bloody saddle - the first blood of the war that I had seen; it was the blood of one of the rebel pickets; and soon I saw the man himself, and aided the surgeon while attending to his ghastly wound; and though there were some secessionists still remaining, it was the hands of loyal people that ministered to him during the few days that he lived, and gave him decent burial when he died."

General Alexander Asboth called upon Unionist citizens of Fayetteville to come forward, then abandoned them to their Confederate neighbors. National Archives.

Asboth sent a dispatch to General Samuel R. Curtis, who commanded the Union Army's Southwestern District of the Department of Missouri, from what he designated as "Headquarters at Colonel Tibbett's." "I am now in Fayetteville. The Stars and Stripes float from its court-house," he reported. "The buildings in the town square are still burning."⁸² Fortunately, the courthouse, Arkansas College, the masonic hall, and a number of homes were still intact.

A Union soldier from Iowa saw the burned buildings, the scattered supplies, and the litter that was strewn everywhere. He happened to pick up a piece of paper and look at it. It was the charter of the Fayetteville masonic lodge, which someone had thrown into the street. This soldier just happened to be a Mason. He took the charter and kept it safely for years, and after the war it was returned to the Fayetteville lodge.⁸³

Later in the day Asboth sent another dispatch from Headquarters House, reporting on skirmishing of the day. "The people having full confidence in your command," he said to his commander, "and looking to you for protection, while the rebels are disheartened by the defeat in Tennessee and by the rapid advance of your troops, I would consider it advisable to hold Fayetteville. The Union men implore it, and promise provisions for our men and forage for the animals. Re-enforced by two regiments of infantry, I will hold the place and surrounding country against all the troops now before us. If ordered to leave, all the loyal people will have to leave with us, just as the Missourians did a few months ago. Some of the leading citizens of the town will see you to-morrow at your headquarters and submit their request to such effect.

"The topographical sketch showing our position and disposition of troops will follow, and will sustain my suggestion as to holding the place. I therefore ask you, general, to grant me and my command permission to remain here."[84]

To the people of Fayetteville General Asboth issued a proclamation, saying that he had come to stop the destruction of the town and to establish the rule of law. He called "upon the loyal citizens of this town to aid me in the furtherance and accomplishment of these objects" and promised to those who "declare their allegiance to the laws of the Union, the protection of its flag."

He could not keep that promise of protection, however. His request to hold the town was denied, and he was ordered to evacuate and move northward. Baxter's vision of never being left among his country's enemies was dashed. Union sentiments of some people had by invitation and promise been openly manifested before Confederate witnesses, and retribution was rightfully to be feared. Asboth had unwittingly done a disservice to the loyal people of Fayetteville. The Union army marched away and left those loyal citizens to their fate.

Vengeance was swift. The next day General McCulloch acted quickly upon a complaint, reportedly from Fayetteville attorney Wilburn D. Reagan. Two or three soldiers arrived at the Tebbetts and the New Hampshire-born attorney who still held Union sentiments was arrested and taken away, southbound toward the Confederate army. Soldiers on Pastor Baxter's doorstep narrowly missed him as he fled into the woods. He was forced to hide out for several days before venturing home again.

> HEADQUARTERS AT COLONEL TIBBETT'S,
> *Fayetteville, Washington County, Ark., February 23, 1862.*
>
> To the Citizens of Fayetteville:
> Sent in command of the advance guard of the United States Army of the Southwestern District, Department of the Missouri, by General Samuel R. Curtis, commanding, I have occupied your town to arrest the wanton destruction of public and private property already inaugurated by the Confederate troops; to sustain those of its inhabitants who have been faithful to the laws; to encourage all who may have temporarily wavered in their duty under the threats of bad and designing men, and to establish the law and order essential to the public weal. While, therefore, calling upon the loyal citizens of this town to aid me in the furtherance and accomplishment of these objects, I at the same time offer to all who may have faltered in their fealty, but who shall now truthfully declare their allegiance to the laws of the Union, the protection of its flag. Deserted fire-sides cannot be guarded, but every house containing a living soul shall have the protection of our power. None, therefore, should depart. Those absent should return.
> General Curtis, the commanding general, desires personally to see and confer with one or two of your leading citizens regarding the welfare of the town, who will be escorted to his headquarters (a distance of a few miles) under guarantees of safety to their persons.
> **ASBOTH,**
> Brigadier-General, Commanding Second Division.

The Battle of Pea Ridge

Although Asboth's Union troops were pulled out of Fayetteville, they did not go far. Confederate General Earl Van Dorn, recently appointed to command the troops in the area, decided immediately to strike as soon as possible. In the following days the Confederate forces came streaming back through Fayetteville on their way to what was expected to be another major battle.

"Most of these troops passed through our town on the 3d and 4th of March, the rear guard remaining all the last night," Pastor Baxter recalled. He described it as "a night not soon to be forgotten by me, as it witnessed the conflagration of our beautiful College building, the scene of so many useful and pleasant hours. Having escaped the torch during the retreat of Price and M'Culloch, some ten days before, we had hoped that it would be spared, but we were doomed to disappointment; the night was clear and cloudless, not a breath of air was stirring, and, as the smoke curled skyward in the calm of midnight, this shrine of learning, the abode of peace, fell a sacrifice to the fierce spirit of war and destruction."

Someone else burned the Washington County Courthouse in the center of Fayetteville town square. "The Courthouse... was burned one night by a crazy Confederate soldier," wrote the slave Adeline Blakely. The man had gone into the cupola on a cold night and, to warm himself, built a fire. Before long he had to be rescued from his own flames.

"The old men in the town saved him," Adeline continued, "and then put him in the county jail to keep him from burning other houses. Each family was to take food to him and they furnished bedding. The morning I was to take his breakfast, he had ripped open his feather bed and crawled inside it to get warm. The room was so full of feathers when I got there that his food nearly choked him. I had carried him ham, biscuits and a pot of coffee."[85] Fortunately, the long time court clerk, Presley Smith, had taken the precious county records and hidden them in a cave. As a result those records are still available today.

The great struggle came only about thirty miles north of town. On March 6 and 7, 1862, the Confederate and Union armies fought the battle of Oak Hills / Wilson's Creek. The sounds could be heard with fear and trembling in Fayetteville. Marian Tebbetts said they could hear "the muffled boom of artillery. A dully, deadly boom–m, boom-m, that died away in an answering echo.... Sometimes there was a clattering, indescribable sound that might have been musketry. Anyway, Fred Zellner, our music teacher, listened and heard in it the motif of a march which he wrote, while the battle was on, built on the refrain from a martial sound that drifted in.... People listened with strained ears, and marveled and wept. All day the terrible detonation with its sobbing echo drifted in and people stood with faces to the north, seeing nothing, but waiting, just waiting, for that endless boom, boom."[86]

Baxter remembered the same thing. He described the situation in Fayetteville in depth: "The quiet which reigned...was soon broken by the roar of artillery, which told that the battle had begun. Thus passed Thursday and Friday: on Saturday morning the news was...the contest was said to be fearful, the slaughter on both sides immense; still the advantage was with the South; Price had got between the enemy and Missouri, and all hope of escape was cut off, the invaders would never return save as exchanged prisoners.

"About ten in the morning came the news of the charge made by the mounted Texan regiments, under M'Culloch and M'Intosh, upon the Federal batteries; the carnage was fearful, and an officer of distinction on the Southern side was reported killed; no one conjectured who it could be. Then the report came that a carriage was coming containing a wounded officer....

"Soon the carriage came in sight; I went across the square to inquire whose body it contained, and was informed that it was a wounded man belonging to one of the Texan regiments. I had seen enough of the treatment of common soldiers to know that this could not be so; the carriage kept on toward Fort Smith, and we soon learned that it contained the body of the famous Ben M'Culloch.

"This was unexpected and startling; matters began to wear a serious aspect; and, just after nightfall, hearing a wagon from the direction of the battle-ground passing my door, I went out to make some inquiries, and found that it contained the body of Gen. James M'Intosh, who fell nearly at the same time M'Culloch.

"The body was taken into the house of an acquaintance of mine; I entered, and there he lay, cold and stark, just as he was taken from the spot where he fell; a military overcoat covering his person, and the dead forest leaves still clinging to it. His wound had not been examined; I aided in opening his vest and under-garments, and soon found that the ball had passed through his body, near, if not through, the heart....

"Returning home from the sad scene I heard the sound of a horse's feet coming down the road from the battle-field; soon horse and rider came into view, both evidently much jaded. I hailed him, and asked the news from the fight; he replied by calling me by name, and I soon found it to be one of our citizens [Thomas M. Gunter], well known to me, an officer in the Confederate army, but just before the breaking out of the war a strong Union man....

"'How is the contest going?' said I. He replied: 'We have them all surrounded; but just before I left a movement was made by our troops to let them get away if they wished to do so. Orders were given to our regiment for every man to take care of himself. Our friend Wilson's son, a lad of fourteen, had his leg shot off, and I thought I would come and let the father know the condition of the son. A terrible time it was, I tell you; their men were vastly better drilled than ours; even when under fire they moved with as much precision as on parade-ground, but ours broke ranks often. Moreover, you know I was a member of the Convention, and it would not do for me to be taken, and so I am here.'

"A few officers came in during the night, and a Confederate surgeon [Dr. Thomas J. Pollard], whom I well knew, when I met him the next morning, said that they were badly beaten; 'the very earth trembled,' said he, 'when their infantry opened fire upon us.' About 10 o'clock on Sunday morning the army, which a few days before had passed my house so exultant and confident of an easy and complete victory, came back; but was an army no longer."

Within hours a flood of humanity came through Fayetteville. It was a defeated Confederate army, going south to save itself. Marian Tebbetts witnessed the procession: "The comers from the battle field grew in number....soon the rout of a defeated army was on the town," she recalled. "There are no words to tell of the dissolution of those men, hungry, sick, wounded, disillusioned, desperate. Mother had Harris take tubs of water to the gate, where we children handed it out by gourd and cupsful which the men drank greedily, some lying down by the tubs as if the acme of desire had been reached... For days that stream of suffering humanity flowed by, without arms, blankets, many without hats, everything thrown away that impeded flight.... The place was overrun. Exhausted men fell within the line of the fence, thankful for a corner in which lie and not be trampled. The porches were covered. All night could be heard their groans and curses and prayers....

"In time the town settled down to quiet, sullen and angry. The southern sympathizers who could get away were gone. Those who could not get away were resentful. The town had been burned, denuded, sacked by contending armies, and it was hungry. Even the well-to-do were needing the bare necessities of life...."[87]

Baxter watched the event as well: "[N]ow the army was a confused mob, not a regiment, not a company, in rank, save two regiments of cavalry, which, as a rear guard, passed through near sundown; the rest were a rabble-rout, not four or five abreast, but the whole road about fifty feet wide perfectly filled with men, every one seemingly animated by the same desire to get away. Few, very few, had guns, knapsacks, or blankets; every thing calculated to impede their flight had been abandoned; many were hatless, and the few who had any thing to carry were those who had been fortune enough to pick up a chicken, goose, or pig; if the latter, it was hastily divided so as not be burdensome, and the usual formalities of butchering and taking off the bristles were dispensed with.

"Very few words were spoken; few of them had taken any food for two or three days; they had lost M'Culloch, M'Intosh, Slack, Reeves, and other officers of note, and, in a word, they were thoroughly dispirited. And thus, for hours, the human tide swept by a broken, drifting, disorganized mass, not an officer, that I could see, to give an order; and had there been, he could not have reduced that formless mass to discipline or order. Many called in with piteous stories of suffering from hunger, and were relieved as far as our means would permit; but these soon failed, and all we could furnish was pure water."

Fayetteville men were in the battle at Pea Ridge, and their stories came back home. Erastus Stirman was promoted for bravery. Washington Wilson's boy, probably Alfred, was killed. Baxter, without naming him, noted that he was "a noble Union boy, had his leg torn away by a cannon-ball at the Pea Ridge fight, and bled to death - dying in a cause he never approved."

After the defeat at the battle of Pea Ridge the Confederacy all but abandoned Arkansas. Arkansas troops were sent east of the Mississippi River to fight in Tennessee and Mississippi, leaving the state almost defenseless. No troops were sent from east of the Mississippi to fight on the west side of the river. Arkansas had to defend itself, with small help from Texas and Louisiana regiments. Fortunately for Confederate Arkansas, the Union command had the same policy, resulting in a corresponding weakness in Northern forces west of the river. Neither Washington nor Richmond was willing or able to devote the resources necessary to obtain victory in Arkansas.

Fayetteville spent the summer and fall of the year 1862 in limbo, permanently occupied by no one but subject to unexpected temporary occupations by patrols from both sides.

"So frequent were the visits from both parties," wrote Baxter, "that we often found it difficult to determine whether we were under Jeff. Davis or Lincoln rule. Sometimes we were under neither.... The frequency of those changes rendered the citizens of different views extremely tolerant of each other; neither party knew how long the other might be in the ascendancy; and though the warmth of former friendship was neither felt nor expressed, the bitterness of past enmity was, if not forgotten, at least restrained."

Robert Graham, the Campbellite minister who had come to Fayetteville at the people's request and established Arkansas College, could stand it no longer. Feeling he was no longer safe, and that he could not yet take his family with him, he left for Union lines in Missouri. His family went later.

Pastor Baxter stayed on, teaching a few children in what had been a military kitchen, and tending to what little was left of his congregational flock. He felt he could not leave. "Summer passed quietly by; every day marked by a Sabbath-like stillness, and our late flourishing little city presenting almost the desolation of a desert," he wrote. "Schools and institutions of learning broken up, churches abandoned, the Sabbath unnoted, every thing around, indeed, denoting a rapid lapse into barbarism, all trade at an end, nearly all travel suspended, the comforts of life nearly all gone, the absolute necessaries difficult to be obtained, altogether made a picture difficult to be realized in a country which has not been made the scene of war...."

The Confederate Conscription Law

After the tranfer of Confederate troops to east of the Mississippi and the withdrawal of Union troops back into Missouri, the situation became desperate. General Thomas C. Hindman was appointed to defend Arkansas, but he had almost no army. He solved the dilemma in two ways, each one of which was to have great consequences. First, he mercilessly applied the recently passed draft law. Second, he issued a call for exempt and non-military age citizens to organize themselves into guerrilla bands to fight the Federals.

The Confederate Congress on April 16, 1862, had passed the first conscription law in American history, requiring that every white, male residents aged 18 to 35 years[*] to go into the military. There were exemptions for government workers, teachers, ministers, druggists, and those with trade skills, and for owners or overseers with twenty or more slaves to supervise. Hindman relentlessly applied the law. *Every* man of suitable age *must* join. His tactics were unpopular in the state, even among Confederates, but he raised an army where none previously existed. Men were forced either to join the Rebel army or flee.

The Confederate Congress later extended the ages subject to conscription to 18 to 45, and still later to 17 to 50. Unlike the North, substitutes were not permitted.

Confederate recruitment in Fayetteville began again. Under the leadership of Colonel William H. Brooks, who had turned over command of his battalion from the previous summer to fellow townsman Ras Stirman, a new regiment designated as the 34th Arkansas Infantry was raised from northwest Arkansas. Five of its ten companies were raised in Washington County.

The first company in the 34th Infantry, later designated as Company A, was formed June 16th in Fayetteville by attorney Thomas M. Gunter, the once Unionist delegate to the secession convention a year before. But times had changed; Gunter was loyal to his state and his people. Later in the summer he was lieutenant colonel of the regiment, second in command to Brooks.

In Gunter's company were enlisted the ever-enlisting John Brandenburg, "R.W. Calfee," who perhaps was Randolph Calfry, and the plasterer Hugh Glass. The First Sergeant was F.G. Watson. The ever-present Williford brothers, Nelson and Henry, joined once again, likely because they were compelled to do so. John Perkins, John Wilson and James K. Wilson also enlisted. So also did young Christopher Columbus Hart.

Another company of recruits was formed on June 20th by Captain Samuel Smithson, which later became Company C. This unit attracted Robert Hodges, Mathew McGarrah (the son of William), H. J. McRoy, First Lieutenant John O. Parks, and Corporal Isaac Taylor. James Pollard was in the same company. The saddler Jefferson Dunlap became a corporal. The wagon maker William Elliott was a private. James Hensley joined Company H. James Moore was the regimental commissary sergeant. Solomom Ward, who may have been S.M. Ward of the census, was in the regiment.

James R. Pettigrew was captain of Company K. He was later promoted to major and then onto lieutenant colonel. The company was formed in Fayetteville on August 5th. "This beautiful valley was a military camp," he said later. "Peaceful pursuits had been abandoned, and all was busy preparation for the inevitable conflict.... {T}he Thirty-fourth...was organized.... The hot blood of youth coursed in our veins then, and the pomp and circumstance of glorious war was hailed with delight. The enemy was approaching; patriotism and desire to defend homes and firesides was at fever heat....."[88]

Pettigrew's next-in-commands were First Lieutenant M. C. Duke, Second Lieutenant Benjamin F. Boone, and Third Lieutenant A. Wilson. James Henry of Fayetteville, and Isaac and Henry Marhsall, who lived just north of town, enlisted. So did James W. Smith, who may have been one of the Fayetteville Smiths, Jonathan Osburne, and another John Wilson.

Americus Rieff, who had captained a company from Fayetteville at Oak Hills/Wilson's Creek, enlisted in the 6th Arkansas Cavalry on May 22nd in Washington, Arkansas. This unit, however, was usually called Monroe's First Arkansas Cavalry. Rieff was immediately elected Captain of that company, and later became Major and Lieutenant Colonel of the regiment. Fayetteville merchant James T. Sutton joined the 15th Arkansas Infantry in McRea's battalion. Dentist J.R. Palmer a company of guerrillas that plagued Union toops in northwest Arkansas for the remainder of the war.

Pastor Baxter complained about the hypocrisy of two Fayetteville attorneys, Alfred M. Wilson and Wilburn D. Reagan. These men, he said, were first and boldest to speak for secession, but they would risk neither their abundant wealth nor their own blood for the cause. This apparently did not go unnoticed among some of the townspeople. Turnabout, however, is fair play. Baxter's good friend Jonas Tebbetts, 41, notably did not join the military of the cause he so warmly supported. Nor, for that matter did William Baxter himself, who, also at 41 years of age, could have done so had he really wanted. He didn't.

By the end of the summer the men of military age in Fayetteville were gone. Judge David Walker, once he became a Rebel, endorsed the Confederacy will all his heart and never let go of it. He was optimistic for the future. "The mountain counties...have turned out nearly every man for duty," he wrote on August 29, 1862. "We have quite a formidable force. The Missourians still pour in by hundreds... God grant that we may be able to raise a force sufficient to protect us. Shurly this war cannot last long."[89]

The rigid enforcement of the Confederate conscription law had two effects. On the one hand, it forced the reluctant and neutral people into the Rebel Army. On the other hand, it forced the true Union men to flee their homes and go northward to U.S. lines in Missouri. W.C. Peerson with backwoods eloquence stated his plight. "I was borned in Washington County on the 23rd day of March 1844," he wrote. "I lived with my Parance until about the age of 18. In the year 1862...I was forced by the Rebels to leave my home and take sides with them or go North to the Federal Army and I took my choice to go North."[90]

There were many other such Unionists in northwest Arkansas, including Fayetteville. Without having loaded their belongings into a wagon or having taken a single step down the road, they found themselves living in a new country not of their choosing. What had once been patriotic loyalty was now treasonous disloyalty, and the transition to new circumstances was difficult or impossible for them to deal with.

In the spring of 1862, the refugees began to appear at Cassville. Captain Marcus LaRue Harrison of the 36th Illinois Infantry was the quartermaster of the Federal garrison at Cassville. He liked these Arkansas men who had given up their homes for the Union. When he was authorized to raise a company for the 6th Missouri Cavalry, he decided to fill the enlisted ranks with them. When the quota was quickly filled, the idea emerged for form an entire regiment from this pool of manpower.

Many Yankee officers did not agree with the 32-year-old Harrison's enthusiasm for these men. A regiment of Union men from seceded Arkansas was, many Northerners thought, just a plain bad idea. The belief was commonly held that such men had divided loyalties and in the final analysis would not fight as soldiers must. "There are officers in the army," Bishop wrote later, "who knowingly shook their heads at the project, and prophesied nothing but failure."[91]

Yet others felt quite differently. Brigadier General Egbert B. Brown, the commander of the District of Southwest Missouri, and Missouri Military Governor John S. Phelps were instrumental in getting the regiment approved in Washington, D.C. Finally, on June 16, 1862, the War Department issued a special order to Captain Harrison, stating that "the Secretary of War hereby authorizes you to raise a regiment of cavalry from the loyal men of Arkansas, to be completed by the 20th of July, and to be mustered into service, clothed, mounted, and armed at Springfield, Missouri, by the United States government. The regiment will be mustered into service for three years or the war...."[92]

Meanwhile, Arkansas men kept coming into Cassville. On May 10th, eleven men led by Thomas J. Gilstrap came to the Federal picket line. Four days later was the arrival of Thomas Wilhite and his thirty men. Then on June 20th, a hundred and fifty men from Washington County rode in under Fayetteville teacher Thomas J. Hunt. These men two years before had been officers in the second battalion of Washington County's 20th Arkansas Militia. Harrison made them officers in the First Arkansas Union Cavalry. George W.M. Reed was made a second lieutenant. Daniel Jones, a miller, was made a sergeant in Company B. Major Thomas J. Hunt afterward estimated that 500 to 800 men of Washington County served in the Union Army.[93] It is clear that Fayetteville had a fair representation in that number.

In October Jonas Tebbetts came into town under a heavy guard of Union soldiers. After the death of General Ben McCulloch he had been released and permitted to leave. Now he collected his family, and they left behind their home and went north to Union lines in Missouri. Mariah Graham and her children went with them, as her husband, Robert, had escaped northward months earlier. Upon reaching St. Louis, Jonas and Marian Tebbets decided that they would never move back to Fayetteville.[94]

Others were leaving Fayetteville, too. It was a dangerous place to be. J.D. Walker, who was held as a prisoner of war in St. Louis, heard that his wife, Mary, the daughter of David Walker, had left town. "I learned a short time ago with great satisfaction that you had left Fayetteville and gone below," he wrote on November 29, 1862.[95] Once exchanged, he himself joined his wife and went to Texas.

In July Thomas Gunter was captured while recruiting Confederate soldiers, and was later paroled and returned to active service. During October Confederate soldier Peter Van Hoose was captured near town by federal troops of the First Arkansas Union Cavalry. He was sent to Springfield, Missouri, where he remained until his death in March 1865 at the very end of the war. He left a wife, Adeline, and three young children under the age of ten years.

The Battle of Prairie Grove

The Union and Confederate armies marched and counter-marched through the fall of 1862. The First Arkansas Union Cavalry was stationed at Elk Horn Tavern, the site of the battle of Pea Ridge, hoping to reclaim Fayetteville for the Union. The 34th Arkansas Confederate Infantry was marched around northwest Arkansas, hoping to keep Fayetteville within the Confederacy.

Again, the talk of an imminent great battle was everywhere. The Rebels, however, were not ready for it. Clem McCulloch of Company B, 34th Infantry, wrote that on "October 8 we learned that a scout of Federals was bearing down on us with the determination of taking us in, as we had no arms. We packed up hastily, and were soon moving toward the south. Before we reached Fayetteville it began to rain, and continued to pour down, and we continued to step until we had crossed the White River and came to a halt at Judge David Walker's place, where we stopped for the night.

"It continued to rain and Col. Brooks had issued an order that no baggage was to be unloaded, and, wet, tired and hungry, we stood up and took the rain until daylight. We did not do a thing but burn every rail around Judge Walker's lots and a quarter of a mile around his corn field. Judge Walker's house was full of officers and men, as was also his barn and every building that had a semblance of a roof, but Capt. Wythe Walker stayed with his company, although within 200 yards of his father's door. The rain ceased about daylight, and we unloaded the wagons and had breakfast and rested until noon.

"When Judge Walker got up in the morning and saw his horses and fattening hogs roaming around [because the fences were gone], he smiled and said he had plenty of Negroes to make more rails. We resumed the march soon after noon." They went into camp at a place called Spadra.

General Hindman visited the camp of the 34th and issued arms. McCulloch added a chilling note to his story. "While in camp here," he wrote, "Dr. Welch got Bill Moore of Company B to sharpen his knives and scissors and put them in a condition to cut off our legs and arms in a scientific manner when occasion demanded." Bill Moore was a Fayetteville tailor, whose professional implements were changed to the needs of war.

Hindman himself rode into Fayetteville about October 17th with his staff and conferred with his commanders. The battle was nearing, but it was not yet to occur. The Confederates rode away and left the town open to the next soldiers who happened to enter.

The Union Army was not far behind. "On the night of the 27th of October, 1862, Gen. Schofield was reported to be near our town," wrote Pastor Baxter. "When day dawned we found our town in possession of a tired and hungry army; and the soldiers, thinking that they had at last got down into Dixie, began to help themselves; considering every house the dwelling of a foe, all fared alike....

"My yard was soon stripped of poultry, my house was filled with soldiers, and we were feeding them as rapidly as we could; some few of them, who had been down on a scouting party, knew me, and their presence was valuable for a time; but other hungry crowds came, and many of them I have no doubt thought that they were cleaning out a secessionist, and did it with a good will; and while I was doing my best to feed as many as the kitchen would hold, and sending them away to have their places filled by others, if possible hungrier still, a number went to the back part of the smokehouse, pulled off some of the planks, and appropriated every thing they could lay hands on."

A newspaper reporter was with this army. Under the dateline of October 29, 1862, from Fayetteville, "Our Fayetteville Correspondent" in the November 7, 1862 issue of *The New York Herald*, reported on what he saw. "The conscription here has been perfect. There is not a man or boy left able to bear arms, and I am informed that the balance of the state is in the same condition. Most of the families of the conscripts have left, so that the town is almost deserted. Fayetteville is a lovely place, and the larger portion of the inhabitants were persons of taste and refinement and a liberal share of wealth. There were many large mercantile establishments fitted up elegantly, and an immense amount of business was transacted. Now there is not a solitary place of business in operation. Before the rebels left they cleaned out every dollar's worth of goods that was worth transportation. Most of the families left their furniture behind, and some of them even their cooking utensils." There were "naked chimneys and blackened ruins" around town. The Union troops also marched away, leaving Fayetteville again unoccupied.

By the first week of December it was clear that there would indeed be a battle. There were two Union armies in the area, one southwest of Fayetteville under General James G. Blunt, and the other in Missouri under General Francis Herron. Hindman decided that he could defeat either of those armies individually, but not combined as one. Herron was marching rapidly southward to reinforce Blunt and unite the armies. Hindman hit upon the plan of attacking Blunt, defeating him, then turning around and attacking Herron. It was one of those schemes that if it works, the general is a genius, and if it doesn't, he is an idiot.

Herron's southbound Union troops approached Fayetteville on the evening of December 6th. 'When I reached home," Baxter wrote of that day, "I found a cavalryman with drawn saber standing at my gate, and learned from him that he belonged to advance guard of Gen. Herron's army, who had given orders to guard every house in the place, so that no citizen might be disturbed as the main body of the army passed through. In a few minutes every house in the line of march was similarly protected, and many heart-felt thanks were expressed for the considerate care manifested by this young and gallant General. Soon his cavalry swept through town in haste to reenforce Gen. Blunt...."

Herron's infantry marched in about midnight. The exhausted men were permitted to fall out of their line of march in the town. Union people brought water and tea to the soldiers.[96] Many slept anywhere they could while others warmed themselves from the severe frost of that night. They "seized any thing and every thing that was combustible- fences, outbuildings, whatever came to hand - and soon hundreds of camp-fires were blazing."

"Just before the Battle of Prairie Grove," recalled the slave Adeline Blakely, "the Federal men came through. Some officers stopped and wanted us to cook for them. Paid us well, too. One man took little Nora on his lp and almost cried. He said she reminded him of his own little girl he'd maybe never see again. He gave her a cute little ivory handled pen knife." The soldier asked Elizabeth Blakely to keep his pistols with her until after the battle. She reluctantly agreed, but he never came back to get them. She assumed he did not survive the conflict. The battle which shortly began, she recalled, "sounded just like popcorn from here in Fayetteville."[97]

Union General Francis Herron ordered guards at every house to prevent his soldiers from harassing the citizens and the property of Fayetteville. National Archives.

After a few hours the soldiers marched out of town, headed southwesterly toward Prairie Grove. The people of Fayetteville were again filled with apprehension. Local soldiers were going to be on both sides of this fight. The fate of the town hung in the balance. "The calm and silence of that lovely Sabbath morning were soon broken by the roar of cannon, which told that the strife had begun," wrote Baxter from his vantage point in town, only a few miles from the site of battle. "The smoke of the battle was visible, and even the rattle of musketry at times reached our ears. For hours the contest raged till about two in the afternoon, when the firing slackened for a time. About four it was renewed with greater violence than before; we knew that the final struggle had come, but knew not at that time on which side the advantage lay....

"The few Union families remaining were greatly excited during the day; a fearful battle was raging in hearing, nay, almost in sight; the Union army was in the heart of an enemy's country, and if defeated there was little hope of its escape, and in case of a retreat it was fully expected that there would be a running fight through the town.... When the sounds of battle ceased our anxiety was not relieved; we knew the conflict was over, but knew not yet whether the brave little band, which had marched by ere the sun of that day had risen, were victors or vanquished. About midnight two men from a cavalry regiment which was in the advance in the morning,[*] came to my house and reported that their regiment had been surprised by the enemy under Marmaduke; that their train was captured, and many of their companions taken prisoners; that they had escaped on foot, and supposed that the day had gone against the Federals.

"The next morning came, and the first sight that met my eyes was calculated to confirm my worst fears. I saw down the street several pieces of artillery, and the heads of the horses which drew them turned northward, and my heart sank within me as I saw the proof, as I deemed it, of disaster and retreat. But my gloom was soon turned to gladness; I hurried down and found that the artillery was for the defense of the town, which was to be henceforth a military post...."

The battle had been hard fought on both sides. "My curiosity to see a battle is satisfied," wrote Union Army chaplain Francis Springer of the Prairie Grove. "I am quite willing that my demise from earth shall come ere my eyes behold or my nerves & moral sensibilities be smitten by another sight so shocking. Sublimity & grandeur of mortal combat are qualities of war I do not care to appreciate. I will not train my heart that my moral nature shall be perverted to a taste for carnage. War is an avenging hell...."[98]

Though perhaps a tactical stalemate, the battle was a strategic victory for the Union. When it was over, Hindman took what remained of his army and headed south.[99] Over the hours and days news of friends and loved ones reached town. The First Arkansas Union Cavalry had been overrun at the beginning of the battle and had fled in panic, disgracing the Arkansas men who fought for the Union. Those who had predicted that Arkansas Unionists would not fight felt self-satisfied in the result.

This was most likely the First Arkansas Union Cavalry, which had many Fayetteville men.

Charles Whiting "White" Walker of Fayetteville was a Lieutenant in the 34th Arkansas Confederate Infantry, who experienced the carnage at the Battle of Prairie Grove. Shioh Museum.

The 34th Arkansas Confederate Infantry had been in the thick of the battle. Of four hundred men engaged in the fighting, fifteen were killed and sixty wounded. Clem McCulloch wrote that "[o]ur men went into battle firmly believing that we would win and that peace would follow soon. This was a hard fought battle, and many of our best men went down to rise no more and many others were maimed for life."

Captain James R. Pettigrew of Company K of the 34th described the day: "The stillness of the morning was broken by the clash of arms.... The battle of Prairie Grove, while of short duration, will compare, perhaps, with any fought during the war in fierceness and desperate gallantry. The rattle of musketry often rose above the roar of artillery, and the bright sunlight gleamed from bayonets.... [I]t was the logic of fate that Brooks' regiment received its first shock of battle, and baptism of blood, almost on the very spot of its origin.... Brooks' regiment can well claim to be the child of Prairie Grove. It had its origin here, and aided in making its fields and groves historic..... Gen. Hindman's army were subjected to the trying ordeal of turning their faces from home and loved ones" and retreating southward.[100]

The 34th suffered painful losses. Lieutenant Benjamin F. Boone was wounded and taken to a church at Cane Hill that was converted into a hospital. There he died three months later. James Pollard, the son of Dr. Wade Pollard, was killed. Lieutenant M.C. Duke was wounded, as was Lieutenant Wilson. Nelson Williford was mortally wounded and soon died.

As it marched away in the snow, defeated and disheartened, Hindman's force almost disintegrated. It would be three years before these men of the 34th would see home again, if ever. A good many in the conscript army had had enough of this war. Desertions were

The Will of Lieutenant Benjamin F. Boone

Lt. Benjamin F. Boone practiced law in Fayetteville for a time. When he married he moved to a new home near Elkins. His first battle was Prairie Grove, where he was wounded and died three months later. He left a will in the form of a letter dated August 2, 1861.

"Beloved wife:
"On tomorrow I start for the war camp of General Ben McCulloch near Springfield, Mo. Should I arrive in time for the battle at Springfield, and it is deemed necessary I may engage in the fight, and should I fall, remember it will be for your and our children's liberty and the freedom of our country - and it is a holy and just cause, humbly relying upon the God that protects the right. I commit myself now to His keeping, trusting that He will do all things well.

"Should I never return, my will and pleasure is that a portion of the property over which God has placed me as steward should be sold, sufficient to pay my indebtedness - the remainder to be carefully husbanded for the mutual benefit of yourself and our children.... That the children should all receive a good English education and be reared in the fear and admonition of the Lord.

"Fare thee well, and should we meet no more on earth, then are thee well till we meet to part no more in the world of endless light.
"Most affectionately, B.F. Boone.
"P.S. Should it become necessary to have this will acted upon, my pleasure is that my brother, Lafayette, or Leroy B. Cunningham, should attend to the matter."
(Nora Boone Carlisle, "A Letter of Lieutenant Boone, C.S.A., *Arkansas Historical Quarterly*, Vol. 3, 1944, pp. 64-65.)

epidemic, and included Henry Williford, who left the army and took his dead brother home.

Pastor Baxter does not reveal their names, but he described the return of James Pollard and Nelson Williford. "Their bodies were brought home for interment, and it is said to look upon their noble forms, both pierced through the heart by the messengers of death," he wrote, "and it was sad beyond expression to witness the agony of a mother's heart as she kissed again and again the cold lips of her proud boy, her first-born, as she clung to his lifeless form, refusing almost to be separated by death."

Fayetteville, Arkansas, was paying a fearful price for this Civil War. The town was largely destroyed. Many people had fled. The men were being killed. Unfortunately, the war still had years more to go.

"One vast hospital."

The tidings of war came flooding into Fayetteville within hours of the fighting. Men wounded in every conceivable and inconceivable way were brought in by the hundreds, overflowing every church and public building and many homes. "The joy of victory...was soon saddened by the usual attendants of success upon the battle-field," wrote Pastor Baxter. "The ambulances, with their mangled and bleeding freight, began to arrive, and groans of agony extorted by every inequality of the road over which they passed were heard. Many of the slightly wounded, supported by a friendly stick, or the stout arm of a friend, began to come in, and ere long the town was one vast hospital....

"During the first few days after the battle many of the severely wounded died; and to me it was a sad sight when, for the first time, I saw a corpse, stark and cold, laid outside of the hospital on the ground, with no covering but a blanket or overcoat, soon to be carried away by the dozen to nameless graves.... My heart sickened, too, when I saw, for the first time, the surgeons carving and sawing the limbs of men like butchers in the shambles; and yet I soon learned that their very coolness was a mercy; there was no time for weakness; that would unnerve the skillful hand when the lives of so many were depending upon their promptness and energy; and indeed it was not long before I could myself stand by the side of one undergoing amputation, and soothe him in the trying ordeal which at first to witness unmanned me....

"I must say, however, that the wounded bore their sufferings like the heroes that they were; no abandonment to grief or useless complaining, but on the contrary, many were calm, and some even cheerful. One noble fellow I well remember; a ball had passed laterally through his breast, a horrible wound, rendering his breathing difficult and painful; the bright red blood, which every feeble cough brought into his mouth, showed that his lungs had been pierced, and

A Description of Fayetteville on December 15, 1862.

Reverend Francis Springer of the Union Army described Fayetteville after the Battle of Prairie Grove. (William Furry, Ed., *The Preachers Tale: The Civil War Journal of Reverend Francis Springer*, pp. 3-4.

"Fayetteville, Arkansas, is - or, more properly, once was, a charming village. In flourishing times previous to the rebellion, its population, I am told, was nearly 2,000 souls. Its inhabitants - if one may judge of them by the remnant yet here - were intelligent, polite, hospitable & happy....

"The numerous workshops & storehouses, now despoiled of their tools & their merchandise, are a sure index of the business activity & thrift formerly prevalent.... Its public buildings were good, - some of them excellent. Fine houses of Christian worship, now used as hospitals for the sick & wounded of our army, were usually well-attended by devout congregations.

"The resident lots are all spacious, measuring from half an acre to four acres in amplitude; & enclosed with fences... well-supplied with fruit trees & fruit-bearing shrubs.... Arkansas College, Fayetteville Female Seminary, & the Fayetteville Female Institute, were institutions of learning that, but for the rebellion, might now be as flourishing as they were in former years... The college & one of the female establishments were totally consumed by fire in obedience to the orders of the rebel chieftain, Ben. McCulloch.... At present there is neither a printing press, a Sabbath school, nor a church-going congregation, - not a school of any kind, nor a lodge-meeting in the place. Fences are torn away, houses broken down or consumed by flames, gardens, fruit-trees, shrubbery & grass plots are marred, mutilated & laid waste. Numerous piles of unsightly ruins mark the sites where hotels, shops & storehouses once invited the concourse of customers. Where, only 18 months ago, order, business & beauty prevailed, dilapidatin & ruin protrude their ungainly forms in every street.

"And the people likewise are wrecked & wasted in spirit, after the fashion of their property... Some of the citizens have fled from the fear of the rebels, & some have gone south to swell the hosts of treason. Among those who remain are some of the oldest & most respectable of inhabitants. These, for the most part, are loyal; but they have been so repeatedly the prey of hostile armies passing through or encamping in the village, that they live in constant dread of all armed men whether loyal or rebel. Soldiering is a trade which develops the worst propensities of depraved human nature. Forcible appropriation, pilfering, rudeness, & obscenity are the slimy traits which the demon of war begets. No wonder that quiet civilians stand in trembling dread of armed friends as well as foes."

yet he was hopeful and cheerful. 'I know,' said he, 'that it is any ugly wound, but I am not going to make a poor mouth about it; I will keep up a good heart, come what may.' And he did keep up a stout heart, and I had the pleasure of seeing him on his feet and able to march again."

The Union Army doctors managed the unmanageable situation as best they could. Dr. Ira Russell, assisted by his son and several surgeons, was in charge of the medical care. There were then ten or twelves hospitals here containing about 650 sick and wounded soldiers.

Dr. Russell's son, upon arrival, was shocked at what he saw. "There has been the most horrible mismanagement here that ever was conceived of," he wrote his mother on December 29th. "I have already seen 5 legs cut off with more yet to be amputated. The stench of the hospitals has been so terrible that I bore it with me in my clothes, it being almost impossible to get it out. We have since we came in power (Tuesday last) put most of the men in beds and bunks, and fixed up generally. The poor fellows are very much pleased with the change."

Five days later his attitude was different. "I see legs amputated every day," he now wrote. "Have got perfectly hardened to them. The doctors are very fine men. We are doing our utmost to help the sick and wounded."

Dr. Russell arrived in Fayetteville on Christmas Day. On the last day of the year he issued a report on the hospitals in town, describing each one. "Many of the men," he stated, "lay on the floor with but one or two blankets, few bunks, rooms very much crowded, air horribly offensive, floors exceedingly filthy, not having been washed." He set about immediately to improve the conditions, and did an excellent job of it.

In a letter to his wife, Dr. Russell's contempt for the Confederates was on clear display. "The country is mountainous and beautiful and healthy. The soldiers fight and take whatever they can get their hands on," he said. "The inhabitants are a lazy, lousy, dirty, ignorant set of vagabonds. We have a great many prisoners and a great many come in and give themselves up to us...."[101]

1863
The Battle of Fayetteville

"This splendid body of cavalry came thundering down Dickson Street."

When the calendar turned over to January 1, 1863, a new era began in American and Fayetteville history. The Emancipation Proclamation issued by President Abraham Lincoln, decreeing that all slaves in rebellious areas shall be then, thenceforth and forever, free. This included the slaves who remained in Fayetteville, and inasmuch as the town was in the hands of Union forces, Lincoln's word was law. The Proclamation said, in part:

"That on the 1st day of January, A.D. 1863, all persons held as slaves within any State or designated part of a State the people whereof shall then be in rebellion against the United States shall be then, thenceforward, and forever free; and the executive government of the United States, including the military and naval authority thereof, will recognize and maintain the freedom of such persons.... And I hereby enjoin upon the people so declared to be free to abstain from all violence, unless in necessary self-defence; and I recommend to them that, in all case when allowed, they labor faithfully for reasonable wages. And I further declare and make known that such persons of suitable condition will be received into the armed service of the United States to garrison forts, positions, stations, and other places, and to man vessels of all sorts in said service. And upon this act, sincerely believed to be an act of justice, warranted by the Constitution upon military necessity, I invoke the considerate judgment of mankind and the gracious favor of Almighty God."[*]

There is no known record of how many slaves were still in town at the time of the Proclamation. There were probably only a few. The Union Army generally freed slaves wherever it went, and this was probably true in Fayetteville. Adeline Blakely, and any other slaves in town on January 1, 1863, were freed that day.

---

* It is interesting to note that on the same day that the Emancipation Proclamation took effect, West Virginia, with President Lincoln's approval, was admitted to the Union as a slave state.

Former Fayetteville educator Robert W. Mecklin, who lived on his farm not far from town, was not appreciative of the new situation. Most of the teachers in town were Northerners, but Mecklin was a thoroughly Confederate education. "The author of this proclamation," he wrote in a letter, referring to Lincoln, "will be looked on with contempt by our posterity as long as an impartial history of our times is read."[102]

The Union occupation of Fayetteville following the battle of Prairie Grove continued into the new year. "Thursday, Jan. 1st, 1863," Pastor Francis Springer of the Union Army of the Frontier noted in his diary. "'63 still finds us amidst the carnage & the ravages of war. Foemen against foemen stand on the same hill-slopes & valleys sodden with the blood of their former companions in arms. This wide & beautiful land once smiling with fruitful fields, & joyous with the hum of industry, now clotted with gore is overspread with destroying armies." Fields, factories, houses & towns are demolished; commerce is stagnant; schools & churches are deserted; hearts once buoyant with hope are they prey or terrors; families once happy are broken up...."[103]

Colonel Marcus LaRue Harrison, previously a captain in an Illinois regiment, became commander of the First Arkansas. Union Cavalry and of the Federal outpost at Fayetteville. He was the most important figure in town during the Civil War. Shiloh Museum.

The town was still overwhelmed with the casualties from Prairie Grove and the efforts to save them, but as the weeks passed the patients died, or recovered, or were sent elsewhere. The number of soldiers assigned to the post diminished as the bulk of the Union Army returned to Missouri. By spring the occupying forces were reduced to a single regiment, the First Arkansas Union Cavalry. It's commander, Colonel M. LaRue Harrison, was appointed as post commander.

This was indeed a unique occupation force in the annals of the Civil War. The First Arkansas was assigned to occupy the very area from which its men were recruited, and it stayed there, with minor interruption, for the remaining two and a half years of the war. Another such prolonged assignment for a regiment during the war is not known.

With this permanent presence of the Federal forces the pendulum of soldier recruitment in Fayetteville swung the other way, with more young men stepping forward to fight for the Union. Harrison accepted recruits for his own First Arkansas Cavalry, and also for the newly organizing First Infantry and First Light Artillery, which he supervised. On February 18th Henry Williford, who had fought for the Confederates at Prairie Grove when his brother, Nelson, was killed, switched sides and joined the Union cavalry. Six days later his other brother, Seneca, did the same. They both served in Company B. So also did Alexander White, who was listed in the 1860 Fayetteville census as a laborer.

Dr. James M. Johnson of Huntsville was appointed Colonel of the new First Union Infantry. Matthew McGarrah, the oldest son of William and Elizabeth McGarrah, who had deserted from the 34th Confederate Infantry, joined this regiment. His younger brother, James McGarrah, joined him in going to the Union cause. Cabinet maker John Buie, shoemaker Jim Carlile, Prussian-born saddler Richard Gartman, wagon maker Dan Jobe, carriage maker Henry J. McRoy, and the 35-year-old, Irish-born plasterer, Roger Fox, all enlisted as privates.

So did Alfred Arrington, the son of the divorced Sarah. Although life-long Southerners, they were Unionists. Alfred enlisted on February 20th, and was assigned as a private to Company D. His story turned quickly tragic as he died a month later on March 23rd. It takes little imagination to conceive of the heartbreak of his mother. The human cost of the war never seemed to end for Fayetteville.

Thomas J. Hunt of the First Arkansas Union Cavalry, who lived just south of Fayetteville, was a captain of one of the companies. He got into some trouble with General Herron for "passing men of my command to their homes without proper authority." This was a serious problem because the men of the regiment served in the very region from which they came. They wanted to be with, and check on the safety of, their families. Hunt, however, was honest and humble in his response to the General's complaint. On January 9, 1863, he answered that "I did pass two men.... I have never received any orders against such. Although it is not proper, it has been a general thing in the Reg't for even line Officers to pass their men ever since I came to it, an error practiced general becomes to common. All I can say General is that I did it...and am sorry for it and hope you will forgive me." This forthright honesty and humility was impressive to Herron. Hunt was not only forgiven but promoted to Major eight months later. In April 1865, just as the war was ending, he was further promoted to Lieutenant Colonel.[104]

It is a great irony that the strong Unionist Reverend William Baxter stayed through the Confederate years of 1861 and 1862, only to leave once the Federal Army occupied the town. After just two months of Union presence he asked Colonel Harrison to permit him and his family to leave with a northbound supply wagon train. The immediate cause of this was that Lieutenant Crittenden C. Wells, a Northerner who had been assigned to the First Arkansas Union Infantry, put a gun to Baxter's head in an argument about taking a fence for a fire. A friendly army can be as dangerous as a hostile one. Baxter had had enough of soldiers and war, destruction, violence and fear.

On February 9, 1863, the Baxter family departed Fayetteville. "Sad, sad, however, was the change in our once beautiful and prosperous inland city," he wrote. "[T]he fences had nearly all disappeared, shrubbery and fruit-trees were ruined, houses were deserted, nearly all the domestic animals killed, dead cavalry-horses lay here and there; the farms, for miles around, were laid waste, the fences having been used to keep up the hundreds of camp-fires which were seldom permitted to go out by night or day; stables were pulled down, out-buildings burnt, and the very spirit of destruction seemed to rule the hour. The contrast between now and better days was most painful; all that was once valued was destroyed or defaced, and, worse than all, the future seemed to have no promise." The Baxters had loved Fayetteville and its people, but they would never live in Fayetteville again.

Sometime during 1863, and probably about this same time that the Baxters left, the store clerk Charles Davenport, his wife Malvinia, and their son Clinton, also headed north. She was from Tennessee, but he was from Philadelphia, and they went back to Pennsylvania until this cruel civil war was over.

David Walker, who had already departed Fayetteville, in March of 1863 traveled to the Confederate capital of Richmond, Virginia. There he met briefly with President Jefferson Davis. He was ushered into the room with Davis along with a dozen others. "The President was seated near the fire at the end of a table covered with papers, a chair near by him," he wrote. "After he was seated, one occupied the vacant seat and entered into conversation, which when over, both he and the President rose, bowed and that visitor retired. The next occupied the vacant seat and so on."

When it was Walker's turn, Davis "invited me to take a seat near which I did and conversed for a short time. When he learned the purport of my visit, he invited me to call again and he would give me a private audience. Upon my next visit we had a fine and rather productive conference, at the close of which he invited me to dine with him at 6, while I accepted." Walker remarked, contrary to the President's image, "The President lives in plain style, by no means equal to many others, is social and easy."[105]

The Battle of Fayetteville

The Union outpost at Fayetteville was in an inherently exposed position militarily. It was fifty miles beyond the nearest Federal base at Cassville, Missouri, and could not be supplied by either train or riverboat. It was difficult to serve by a vulnerable road through enemy territory. The deteriorating condition of the horses rendered it even more isolated. The post could not maintain an effective reconnaissance of the surrounding country, and could neither be quickly reinforced nor rapidly withdrawn. It was an inviting target. Its greatest defense was the corresponding weakness of the Rebels in northwest Arkansas.

Early in 1863 Brigadier General William L. Cabell was appointed to the command of the Confederate forces in northwest Arkansas. "I hope you will move on Fayetteville," Confederate General William Steele wrote to Cabell on March 12th. "My information is that there are only about a thousand men there, and no cannon." Upon receiving the further (though erroneous) information that the Federal troops at Fayetteville were preparing for withdrawal, Cabell decided that the opportune moment had indeed arrived. His reasoning was given in his report after the battle: "Knowing that our good citizens had burdens imposed on them by the Federal troops too grievous to be borne much longer; that it was necessary for me to visit that section of the country, and having been appealed to by citizens, both male and female, to give them assistance, I determined that I would strike there the very first time that I saw the least hope, whether I succeeded in taking the place or not."[106]

Assembling his brigade at Ozark, about 75 miles by road to the south on the Arkansas River, Cabell made ready for the assault. The Confederate expedition against Fayetteville numbered about 900 men.

The Federal post at Fayetteville was not in a prime condition to receive this Confederate attack. Colonel Harrison had under his command the First Arkansas Union Cavalry, the First Arkansas Union Infantry and the First Arkansas Union Light Artillery. The apparent strength, however, was not actually present. When the shooting began, he had about 1,100 men on hand.

Confederate Brigadier General William L Cabell, who commanded at the Battle of Fayetteville on April 18, 1863. Library of Congress.

Rumors were rife that the Rebels would strike at Fayetteville. On April 2nd, Colonel William A. Phillips wrote to Harrison ordering him to be prepared: "Call in the command, and keep it at the post. Throw up earthworks as speedily as possible. Defend yourselves as you see fit, but lose no time.... Put your men in effective shape. Make their position strong. Exert yourself so as not to embarrass me.... I...have confidence in your judgment with *your peculiar command.*"[107] The old Yankee suspicion about Arkansas Union troops is apparent in this "peculiar command" comment. Loyal Arkansas soldiers still had a point to prove to their fellow countrymen - that they could and would fight. Their opportunity to do so was fast approaching.

All things considered, some nine hundred Confederates were attacking about eleven hundred Federals. In an approximately one-to-one attack, it was obviously going to be very tough going for the Confederates, but, as Cabell stated afterward, he had mistakenly expected the Union troops to be in the midst of vacating the town. If this had been true, then the odds could possibly have shifted in his favor. But it was not true. Even as it was, however, Cabell still had two things in his favor - surprise and artillery. If he was to win this

The Confederate Call to Arms, March 28, 1863

To The People of North and West Arkansas:

In obedience to special orders from Headquarters of the Trans-Mississippi District, I this day assume command of all the troops, of whatever kind, in Northwest Arkansas. In doing so, I hope to be able in a short time to rid that section of the state of the presence of an insolent and unscrupulous invader. To do this I must have the hearty cooperation and sympathy of the citizens, and the united and determined effort of the soldier. I bring with me to the task the life-time experience of a soldier, coupled with the zeal of a citizen. Arkansas is the home of my adoption, and that part of it I am assigned to is my favorite locality.

The soldiers of Arkansas have, in the present struggle for independence, distinguished themselves on every battlefield. The record they have made on the bloody plains of Virginia, Missouri, Tennessee and Mississippi have shed a halo of glory around their name, and I know that in defending their homes and families they will maintain the character they have made in other states. I therefore ask every man in Northwest Arkansas, capable of bearing arms, to rally to the defense of their homes and their firesides. Every man knows he owes his country service, and should come forward at once, and enroll themselves beneath their country's flag, and protect their rights and their liberties. Come at once! In war, moments are precious.

Those who betake themselves to arms are expected to do their whole duty; those who remain at home should do theirs. The soldiers must be fed and clothed. I hope that a spirit of industry will pervade all classes; that farms will be cultivated with care; that the hum of the busy wheel will be heard in every household, and that the women of Arkansas will emulate the mothers and daughters of the Revolution. We are engaged in a war with a bitter, unscrupulous and mercenary enemy - our success alone can terminate it. The motto of the enemy is "and Spoliation;" our's is, "Peace - Independence."

We must conquer it. The enemy must be driven from the soil of Arkansas, and beyond the borders of Missouri. The war has now assumed such vast proportions, and is being prosecuted with so much vigor, that it can not, in the nature of things, be of long duration. One united and vigorous effort on the part of the soldiers of Arkansas will expel the invader. He will not return.

W. L. Cabell, Brigadier-General, Commanding Northwest Arkansas battle, he would need to make good use of both.

Cabell's Brigade left Ozark at about three in the morning on Thursday, April 16th, with three days rations and a full supply of ammunition. On Friday they rode till noon, then rested until sunset. In the dark, they made their way toward Fayetteville up the Frog Bayou Road.

Although the Union defenders at Fayetteville were expecting a Confederate attack to occur sometime in the near future, they were not in immediate expectation of it on the evening before it actually occurred. Lieutenant Joseph S. Robb of Company B of the First Union Cavalry returned to town on Friday the 17th, reporting that his scout in the direction of Ozark revealed "no apparent preparations of the enemy to move in this direction."[108] Colonel Harrison took the report at face value. Lacking the horses to maintain a constant mounted patrol, he decided to wait until the next day to send out another scout. Lt. Robb, by a very considerable margin, had missed the very purpose of his scout, returning to his post with a Confederate army only hours behind him.

Throughout Friday night, April 17th-18th, the Confederates closed in on Fayetteville. Moving along the West Fork of the White River, they advanced northward and then westward toward town. A few minutes after sunrise the Confederates encountered the dismounted Union picket just east of town. It was just about sunrise now, about 5:40 a.m., and it was time for the attackers to make their move.

The Rebels quickly overran the picket post, but shots were fired before it was all over. Two Union privates were killed. Private George W. Russell of Company G was captured, identified as having been a Federal spy in the past, and hanged in execution. One or two others were also captured.

Though killed and captured, the guards had nonetheless successfully performed their mission. "The firing of the picket had alarmed the command," Colonel Harrison wrote afterward. General Cabell's element of surprise, so carefully preserved up to this moment, now began rapidly to dissipate.

With the enemy alarmed, the Confederates moved as quickly as possible to get into a position on the south and west side of East Mountain (now called Mt. Sequoyah) to launch their attack. General Cabell, the brigade staff, the artillery and the cavalry reserve turned off the road into town and went northward up a mountain road

This 1850s drawing by William Quesenberry shows Arkansas College on the right, with the traffic before it on what is now called College Avenue. The house on the far left is that f Jonas Tebbetts, which on April 18, 1863, was the headquarters of the Union Army. It faces onto Dickson Street, which is not visible in the drawing. The house second from left is that of William Baxter. These two buildings were the center of the Battle of Fayetteville. The Confederate attack came from East Mountain, which is behind the trees. Washington County Historical Society.

to a fairly flat point overlooking Fayetteville. The men designated for the attack went a little further west, then turned off the road and went northward up a deep ravine to get closer to the Federal positions. Other cavalry went on to the outskirts of town and set up a far left wing on the southeast edge of the city. These movements were not easy or fast. The men had to be brought up and dispositions completed. The time involved in this effort ended what little advantage of surprise still lingered after the firing of the picket.

"The soldiers were still in bed when the first alarm was given," wrote Sarah Yeater, who that morning was in the house left behind by Pastor Baxter.[109] The commotion awakened Federal Lieutenant Elizur B. Harrison, the younger brother of the post commander. "About daybreak on the morning of April 18th," he recalled many years later, "I was awakened by an unusual noise, and hastily dressing, I opened the east door of my room [in the Baxter house] and to my consternation saw near the back of the lot a column of Confederate cavalry. It is needless to say that I hurriedly shut the door and made my getaway through the front door down to College Avenue."

Once out of the house, Lt. Harrison found his brother, the Colonel, coming away from Headquarters House where he resided. Joining him, they hurried together over to the camp of the First Union Cavalry, which lay north up the Telegraph Road. "We found the men getting into their clothing, gathering arms and ammunition," the Lieutenant said, "while the officers were getting the men into order."

Though taken by surprise, Colonel Harrison responded quickly and "had time to get his men in position before the attack was made." Lt. Harrison later said that his brother "at once took command and very quickly the men...were marched to position in the rear of the Tebbetts house and the dense hedge that surrounded it."[110]

Harrison set both the First Cavalry and the First Infantry into motion. He did not know how many men the enemy had, what their troop dispositions were, or what their intentions were. All he could do was react, and he did a good job of it, setting up a main defensive line with protective flanks and a reserve. He ordered "the First Sergeants to personally see that their companies were supplied with ammunition."

The First Cavalry, on foot throughout the battle, was ordered into position to receive the attack. The third battalion (consisting of only two companies) was placed on the right, under the command of Major Ezra Fitch. The second battalion under Lt. Col. Albert W. Bishop and Major Thomas J. Hunt was put on the left. The center, commanded personally by Colonel Harrison, consisted of four companies of the First Cavalry with three companies of the First Infantry in immediate reserve. "Fearing that, not being uniformed, they might be mistaken for the enemy," Harrison put the rest of the infantry (seven companies) in a distant reserve in a sheltered position to the rear under the command of Lt. Col. Searle. Captain Rowen E. M. Mack of Company G of the Cavalry was ordered "to reconnoiter on the right to prevent a flank movement in that direction." Captain Hugo C. Botefuhr and Company C were placed in ready reserve.[111]

During the time of deploying, General Cabell was surely feeling the many frustrations to afflict him that day. It was already apparent that the Federals were not getting their wagons ready to pull out of town, as he had been told. "Our friends," he lamented afterward, "are all too anxious to rid the country of their presence to state things as they really are." Cabell also found what he erroneously estimated to be a good many more Union soldiers than he anticipated, "notwithstanding all previous reports from persons living in Fayetteville to the contrary."[112] The advantage of his hoped-for surprise was now gone, and his artillery was still not ready.

About six o'clock the Confederates made their initial move toward town, charging on horseback "with wild and deafening shouts" out of the ravine and toward Federal Headquarters (at the Tebbetts house) and the Baxter house. This attack was under the immediate command of Colonel John Scott, and included Carroll's Cavalry (under Lt. Col. Lee L. Thomson) and Dorsey's Missouri squadron, (commanded by Colonel Caleb Dorsey).

This "dashing charge," wrote Cabell, "drove the enemy to their pits and to the houses, where they rallied and poured in a dreadful fire with their long-range guns [Whitney rifles]." John M. Harrell, who later served as a Colonel in the brigade but was not present at this battle, wrote that "[i]n the streets Cabell's men met with effectual resistance from the windows, doorways and corners of the houses...." Henry G. Orr of Parson's Texas Cavalry wrote that the attack sent "the enemy seeking protection in and behind houses and some in rifle pits."

Within thirty minutes of the initial attack, Lieutenant William Hughey had his two-gun section of artillery in place and ready for action. It was located on a relatively flat spot on the hillside where it commanded a good part of the Union line, with General Cabell's own battle headquarters behind it. Cabell had a good high position from which to observe the battle unfolding below him. The guns were protected by visibility-obscuring brush and a skirmish line of Texans.

The artillery roared into action, firing canister and shell at the Union positions and causing a great deal of fear among many of the defenders. "Very soon after the first shots were fired a shell hit the jamb of the basement door," Sarah Yeater said of the Baxter house, "splintered it, knocked bricks from the chimney, broke a large kettle containing lye standing on the hearth, and rolled out of sight." According to Lt. Harrison, this cannonball was a fuse shell which was extinguished when it landed in the lye, preventing the explosion of the shell and sparing the lives of the several women hiding in the room

The Confederate guns focused on the camp of the First Union Cavalry. Cabell wrote that the artillery "did frightful execution in the enemy's camp, driving them out and completely scattering their cavalry for awhile." Colonel Harrison reported that the enemy guns "opened a sharp fire of canister and shells upon the camp..., doing some damage to tents and horses, but killing no men."[113]

"We were using the large brick smokehouse in the rear of the Van Horn lot as an arsenal," said Lt. Elizur Harrison, "and Jim Bell, a private in Company I, was stationed there to notify us if any attempt was made to capture our supplies." One cannon "shot passed over the higher ground and in falling crashed through the body of Jim Bell at the arsenal."

At the commencement of the fight a Federal soldier put his sights on the Confederate artillery commander. Lt. Hughey was wounded in the arm, but was nonetheless able to stay at his post and continue directing his men throughout the morning. "Captain Hughey deserves especial mention," Cabell reported, "for his bravery, skill and energy in the management of his two pieces of artillery." The effect of the intense cannon fire was to cause a considerable fear and demoralization in many of the untried Federal troops. Lieutenant Elizur Harrison stated that at the beginning of the battle it seemed destined to end in defeat for the Union troops.

It was probably about this time that two men from Company A of the First Arkansas Union Infantry broke under the stress of their first battle. Thirty-year-old Private Francis W. Cannon "run and concealed himself," and 18-year-old Private Gilbert C. Luper "was frightened and run when the rebels made their appearance." Corporal Thomas Bingham of Company E of the Infantry and Private Cyrus Barber of Company L of the Cavalry decided that it was time to run for their lives. Colonel Harrison later reported that he had thirty-five men missing, "mostly stampeded toward Cassville during the engagement." He further noted that Lt. Col. Searle and Major Elijah Ham of the First Infantry "did good service in keeping their men in position [in reserve] and preventing them from being terrified by the artillery."

But the fear was not confined to the enlisted men. First Lieutenant Crittenden C. Wells, quartermaster of the First Infantry and the very man who had put a pistol to Reverend Baxter's head, "ran away disgracefully to Cassville, Missouri." At the commencement of the bombardment, at about seven o'clock, Captain DeWitt C. Hopkins of Company I and First Lieutenant William L. Messenger of Company D, both of the First Cavalry, quickly lost hope under the cannon fire. In their minds they exaggerated the number of guns they faced. They went to Colonel Harrison, saying that six artillery pieces had been planted by the Confederates, and that the enemy was flanking them.

"I replied," Harrison reported later, "'How can we retreat; they on horses and we on foot? Would you wish to be disgraced by a surrender?'" The spooked officers said they would not, they all vowed to "fight it out to the death," and returned to their commands. "And right well did they do their duty," Harrison said afterward. In response to the concern about flanking, Harrison directed Lt. Col. Searle of the First Union Infantry to send two companies (one of which was probably Company K) to the left of Lt. Col. Bishop's position. He also directed Captain Randall Smith and Company A of the Union Infantry to report to Major Fitch on the right.[114]

The demoralizing effect of the artillery, and the wavering it caused in the Union defense, was Confederate high tide at the Battle of Fayetteville.

Lt. Col. Albert W. Bishop of the First Arkansas Union Cavalry. Shiloh Museum.

With the Union lines being hopefully softened by the artillery bombardment, Cabell now moved to test the resolve of the Union troops, finding out for himself whether Arkansas Union troops would fight or run. Monroe's Confederate cavalry dismounted and advanced on foot as infantry through the open fields northeast of town toward the Federal left. Lt. Col. Bishop, the Union commander in that section, called Monroe's assault a "bold advance." Lieutenant Harrison called it "a heated skirmish." Monroe's dismounted attack did not break the Federal left, and it was discontinued.

Although the strategic objective of the Confederates was the capture of Fayetteville, the primary tactical target was the Federal headquarters house in the center of the Union line. There was ongoing shooting and maneuvering, and the headquarters was repeatedly but unsuccessfully charged by dismounted Rebels. Bullet holes in interior doors of the house even today mark the ferocity of the struggle there.

Union rifle firepower was overwhelming. General Cabell

The Battle of Fayetteville
April 18, 1863

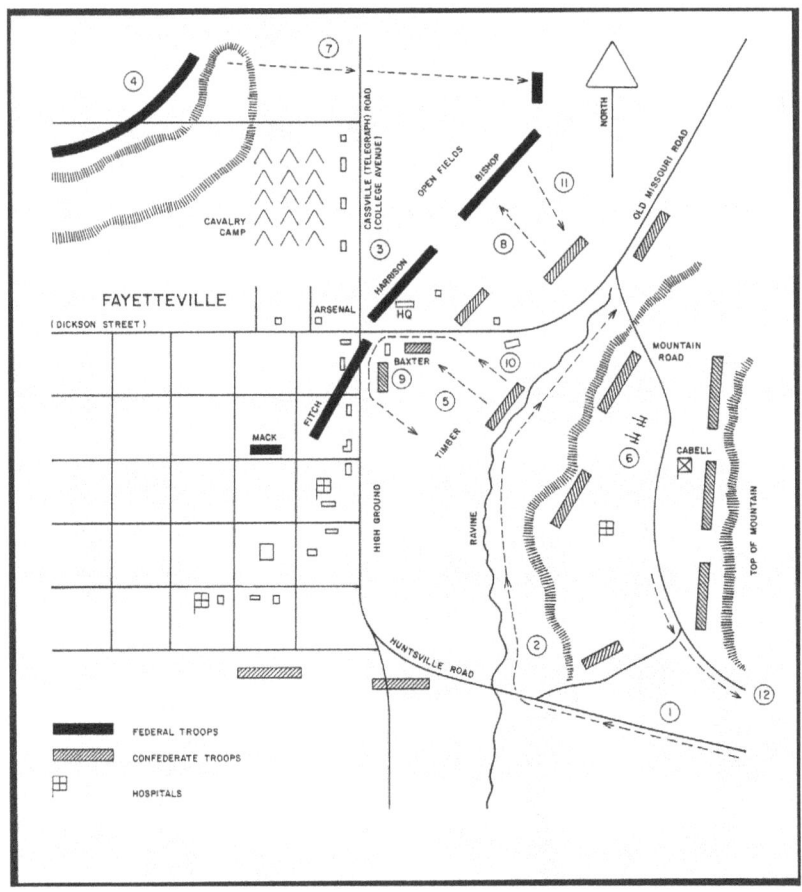

Battle Map Summary

(Numbered paragraphs correspond to numbers on the map.)

   1. 5:40 a.m. The Federal pickets east of Fayetteville are quickly overrun by Confederates under Brigadier General William L. Cabell. Shots alert the Union defenders commanded by Colonel M. La Rue Harrison that an attack is imminent.

   2. Using the ravine running north-south between East Mountain and the town, Confederates move closer to the Federal positions. Cabell sets up his field headquarters and a hospital on the hillside, with artillery to his front and reserves to his rear. Other Rebel troops occupy the

southeastern part of Fayetteville.

3. Harrison establishes a defensive line consisting mostly of the dismounted First Arkansas Cavalry. He commands the center, and places Lt. Col. Albert W. Bishop on the left and Major Ezra Fitch on the right.

4. Most of the First Arkansas Union Infantry, which had no uniforms, is placed out of harm's way behind high ground to the rear. Three companies of Infantry, however, form part of Harrison's center line.

5. 6:00 a.m. Colonel John Scott directs a Confederate mounted charge of Dorsey's Missouri Squadron (under Major Caleb Dorsey) and Carroll's First Arkansas Cavalry (under Lt. Col. Lee L. Thomson). The Union defenders disperse into houses, behind hedges and walls, and into rifle pits, and with their superior muskets bring the attack to a halt.

6. 6:30 a.m. Lieutenant William M. Hughey's Confederate two-gun battery opens fire from East Mountain. It pours in a heavy fire nearly panicking the Federals, but they stand firm.

7. Harrison sends two companies of the First Arkansas Union Infantry to protect the Federal left flank.

8. Colonel James Monroe's First Arkansas Confederate Cavalry makes a dismounted attack in the open fields on the Union left. It fails to break the Federal line.

9. There is fighting in and around Federal Headquarters and the Baxter house between dismounted men from Carroll's Cavalry and Harrison's Unionists. This is the area where the most casualties are inflicted. The Confederates capture the Baxter house, but the Federals hang on to Headquarters and its grounds.

10. 9:00 a.m. Colonel Monroe leads a cavalry charge up the Old Missouri Road (Dickson Street), but runs into heavy defending musket and pistol fire from Federal defenders on the right and in front. The attack fails and the cavalrymen make a left turn and retreat.

11. Lt. Robb of the First Arkansas Union Cavalry leads two companies to within musket range of the Confederate artillery and pours in a heavy fire. With ammunition exhausted, Lieutenant Hughey withdraws his artillery from the battle.

12. The Confederate attack has failed. Desultory fighting continues on, but the battle is essentially over a little after 9:00 a.m. Cabell considers burning the town of Fayetteville as he pulls out, but decides not to do so because of Confederate families there. By noon, the Rebel army is gone.

quickly learned to his chagrin that the Union weaponry was vastly superior to his own. The Federals were "well armed with Springfield and Whitney rifles," and "they poured in a dreadful fire with their longer range rifles." These rifles were one-shot muskets with a rifled, or grooved, barrel interior, which would put a spin on the musket ball, shooting it further and more accurately than the old smoothbore guns. The Arkadelphia guns used by the Rebels, Cabell lamented, were "no better than shotguns."[115] The Confederates had difficulty getting close enough to use their shotguns effectively while always themselves within deadly range of enemy rifles. The Rebels were at a serious disadvantage with their inefficient arms, and, in the final analysis, the disadvantage could not be overcome.

Headquarters House was the center of the Battle of Fayetteville. It is now the home of the Washington County Historical Society. Author's Collection.

The Confederates successfully attacked and captured the Baxter house across the street from Federal Headquarters, taking it early in the battle. It became the anchor of the Confederate center. During the battle it was struck and pierced by more that fifty shot, shell and bullets.

A Confederate hospital was established on a level area of the mountainside the Rebels occupied. The medical team there had plenty of work to do. The Federals, meanwhile, were taking their own losses.

During the battle First Cavalry surgeons, Drs. Amos H. Caffee and Jonathan E. Tefft "were very prompt in sending out their ambulance and directing where they should be driven, doing this while the engagement was still in progress."*

There were various actions in town. The Rebels took possession of the southeast part of town, capturing and destroying a Federal supply train of 10-15 wagons and capturing six escort soldiers. Private James J. Hutchinson was captured at the hospital of the First Union Infantry. Harrison ordered Major Fitch on the right to send a company "to drive in the enemy's pickets at the hospital."

Before long, the Federals were advancing in an attempt to retake the gains of the Rebels. Colonel Harrison reported that "at 8 a.m. our center had advanced and occupied the house, yard, and outbuildings, and hedges at my headquarters; the right wing had advanced to the arsenal, and the left occupied the open field on the northeast of town, while the enemy had possession of the whole hillside east, the Davis [Baxter] place, opposite to, and the grove of, headquarters. This grove was formerly occupied by the building of the Arkansas College."

Harrison decided to try to knock out the Confederate artillery, thereby depriving the Rebels of their best advantage. He sent his brother, Lt. Harrison, with an appropriate order for Lt Col. Bishop. Bishop then selected Lt. Robb of Company L to advance with two companies and try to silence the guns by picking off the individual artillerists with rifle fire.

Things were stalling badly for the Confederates, and Cabell's opportunity to win this battle was fast dissipating. About 9:00 o'clock, Colonel James C. Monroe's cavalry regiment was ordered mounted for a charge at the Union center.

At that moment Union Dr. Seymour D. Carpenter was on the porch of a house on the Cassville Road behind Major Fitch's Federal right wing. "East of the road was a wide wooded ravine, in which, and screened by the timber, the enemy's cavalry formed for the charge," Carpenter recorded. "Suddenly I heard a tremendous yell, then the clatter of the horses, then the toss of their flags, and then they were upon us." The Confederate cavalry attacked uphill on the Old Missouri Road, now known as Dickson Street.

---

* Interestingly, this Confederate hospital is now the very place where the Fayetteville Confederate cemetery is located.

Dr. Seymour D. Carpenter witnessed the Confederate cavalry charge which unsuccessfully sought to break the Union center. Author's Collection.

Dr. Carpenter went on to describe the event: "Major Ezra Fitch, who was in immediate command of the Battalion in front of me, I had always regarded as a dull and stupid sort of man. I particularly disliked him, because he always wore a tall black plume on his slouch hat, but he was something like a tortoise. He required coals to be put on his back before he could get up a move. In the present instance he rose grandly to the occasion. As soon as he heard the yell, he rushed up and down in front of his line, brandishing a revolver in one hand, and the objectionable plume hat in the other, with oaths that would have done credit to the 'army in Flanders,' he admonished his men to stand steady, to reserve their fire until the enemy reached the brow of the hill, and then to 'give 'em hell.'"

Colonel Harrison personally commanded the Federal center where the Confederate attack was aimed. He ordered his men to "fire low, take good aim and be sure to kill a man every time."

Dr. Carpenter continued: "The brow of the hill was about forty yards from the line. In a minute the long line of Cavalry appeared, the Major rushed in front, gave the command to fire, and a sheet of flame from five hundred carbines greeted them; dozens of men and horses went down; I could see the line waver, and the men frantically reining their horses, and swerving to the right and left. They were armed with sabres, and if they had pistols they did not use them. All our men had carbines, and revolvers, and in a minute not a Rebel was in sight, save the killed and wounded.... The Major sped the fleeting guests, with fresh volleys, and then he, and his men began giving assistance to the wounded. Not a man on our side had received a scratch. The whole affair was over in five minutes. It was a most thrilling sight."[116]

Lieutenant Elizur Harrison at the time of the charge was on his way to Lt. Robb to deliver orders from his older brother. He described what he saw: "I saw coming over the rise in front of the Tebbetts house a charge of cavalry so splendid in its bearing, so daring in its onrush, that the memory of it is as fresh in my mind as if it were but yesterday..... [T]hey were met by a fire from the Federal soldiers behind the foundation wall, so deadly that the most heroic could not face it, and turning the corner onto College Avenue, the column moved on and disappeared by way of the lot [to the south of the Baxter House]...."[117]

Meanwhile, Lieutenant Robb was advancing with two companies from the Federal left to move in close upon the artillery "for the purpose of silencing if possible the enemy's battery." Robb formed his men in a field northeast of town. "Their artillerists and guns were out of sight, hidden by the brush," Colonel Harrison later explained, "and I ordered that after the discharge of their artillery my men should aim and fire their rifles about one foot above the blaze of the discharge."

The fire of Robb's Federal skirmish line was effective. The Confederate battery lost one killed and several wounded, plus two horses killed and two wounded. Bishop reported that "the guns were limbered with great speed and hastily withdrawn to play no further part in the events of the day." The artillery fell silent about 9 a.m., not long after Monroe's failed charge.

General Cabell had a different explanation of the withdrawal of the artillery. Earlier he had wanted to move the artillery closer for more effective use but could not do so because he did not have adequate small arms to protect the guns. Now the artillery was withdrawn, he said in his report, because the supply of ammunition was exhausted. Credence is given this statement by Cabell's report a week later that his artillery guns still lacked ammunition. The truth of the matter is probably that the Confederates were indeed running out of ammunition just at the point that Federal rifle fire was getting very hot, and there was no longer any point in hanging around.

Whatever the reason, the artillery fell silent and the only Rebel advantage in the battle was gone. In fact, all the Confederate momentum was now gone, though the attackers persistently hung on to the Baxter house at the center of their line. Both wings had been partially pushed back from this center point. Desultory fighting continued for nearly an hour.

Faced with the reality that his attack on Fayetteville had failed,

Cabell thought about burning the town to the ground. "I could have burned a large part of the town," he said, "but every house was filled with women and children, a great number of whom were the families of officers and soldiers in our service, and I did not deem it advisable to distress them any further, as their sufferings now are very grievous under the Federal rule."[118] Instead, Cabell simply ordered the Confederates to retreat.

The Battle of Fayetteville, Arkansas, was over.

"[T]he rebels retreated," recalled Sarah Yeater, "leaving their dead on the ground.... Nine men dressed in Confederate gray were picked up in the [Baxter] yard and given decent burial in the cemetery.... [O]n examining my room in the cottage we found that two bullets had passed through the mattress where [baby] Charley and I had been lying, the window and chamber set were broken and several bullets had passed through the walls. In the large house many windows were broken and two cannon balls besides numerous bullets had left their marks."[119]

To care for his wounded, General Cabell left behind a medical team under the command of Dr. Algemanus S. Holderness, a 29-year-old physician from Calhoun County, Arkansas. A team of men was detailed to work with Holderness as nurses. The dead and wounded of both sides were collected by the Union troops in Fayetteville. "A wounded Rebel was brought to the porch where I was," said Dr. Carpenter. "He was making loud complaint; his middle finger had been shot off. I hastily dressed the wound, and in a minute or two he dropped over dead. I was quite astounded, but on making a closer examination, found that he had been shot in the abdomen, and had died from internal hemorrhage."

The following day a burial team under the command of Captain William A. Alexander of Company C of Monroe's Regiment was sent back by Cabell under a flag of truce to "get up the dead and wounded." Colonel Harrison responded with a note to Cabell, informing him that "the dead ...have all been decently buried in coffins," and that the wounded "are receiving every attention that men can receive - abundance of medicines, surgical instruments, and subsistence stores having been placed under the control of your surgeons. Rest assured, general, that your wounded shall receive the best of care, such as we would hope to have from you were we placed in a like situation." He also generously returned the Confederate battle flag that had been captured in Monroe's ill-fated charge.

Colonel Harrison was exuberant as the Confederates retreated. The evening after the battle he sent out a preliminary report by telegraph to General Samuel R. Curtis: "Arkansas is triumphant! The rebels...attacked Fayetteville at daylight this morning, and, after four hours' desperate fighting, they were completely routed, and retreated in disorder toward Ozark.... Our stores are all safe; not a thing burned or taken from us." The following day he issued a Victory Proclamation to be read that day at church services.

Federal losses were reported by Colonel Harrison as 4 killed, 26 wounded, 16 prisoners and 35 missing. A thorough study of the records, however, gives somewhat different figures, in part due to wounded men dying and missing men becoming accounted for. More accurate figures are 10 men killed and mortally wounded, 28 wounded but not mortally, and 26 captured. This made a total of 64 Federal casualties, or 6% of the total Federal force. Several of the Union dead from the First Arkansas are now buried at the National Cemetery in Fayetteville.

Meanwhile, congratulations from Union commanders came pouring in to the justifiably self-satisfied Union soldiers of Arkansas. The fact that Arkansas' own Unionist sons had attained the victory over Arkansas Confederates was immediately recognized. General Herron, who had scathingly criticized the First Arkansas Union Cavalry four months earlier, was just as quick to send his compliments: "I must congratulate you on the success of yesterday. It augers well for the future of Arkansas when her loyal troops have beaten the enemy in their first encounter. Such success should encourage us, and I hope soon to see 10,000 loyal men of Arkansas arrayed on the side of the Union. You have nobly sustained yourselves, and deserve a country's gratitude."

The commander of the entire department, General Curtis, added his respects: "Tender my thanks to the soldiers of your command for their gallant conduct in the battle of Fayetteville. You have done nobly. Arkansas vindicates her own honor by repulsing the rebel flag with her own brave sons. Send minute reports, naming the most deserving officers and men."[120]

Rather than receiving congratulations, General Cabell had a much less enviable task of assessing and explaining his defeat. " I did not take the place," he wrote to General Steele, "and if I had with me every man I have on paper, armed as they are [with shotguns], I could have done no more. I made an honest effort to take the place, and have given them a severe blow, and one that will prove to be a good one in the end, as it will curb their utter lawlessness...."[121]

A week after the battle, General Cabell estimated his losses as not more than 20 killed, 30 wounded and 20 missing. The *Little Rock True Democrat* reported 32 killed and 38 wounded. Harrison said not less than 20 killed and 50 wounded Confederates were left in Fayetteville, and that citizens reported to him that many wounded were moving with the command. Dr. Carpenter said 50 to 60 were wounded in Monroe's charge alone. With the incomplete records kept then and available now, about the best that can be said is that the Confederates suffered about 70 killed and wounded and 54 captured. Since many of the captured were also wounded, it is possible only to roughly estimate a total of 100 casualties. This was about 11% of the entire Confederate force.

The best summary of what the Battle of Fayetteville meant for the Arkansas Federals was stated by Lt. Col. Albert W. Bishop of the First Arkansas Union Cavalry. Although always partisan in whatever he wrote, he was indisputably accurate when he stated: "This engagement, though of minor importance as compared with the contests of the Army of the Potomac, or the struggles that have recently culminated in the capitulation at Vicksburg, is not without its significance. It was the first battle of the war in which the loyal men of Arkansas were alone opposed to the organized treason of the State, and gave a very decided reproof to the rebel slander, that the Union men of Arkansas will not fight."[122]

Even more significant than the Unionists claiming that this lesson was taught was the concession of the Confederates that the lesson had been learned. The *Little Rock True Democrat* on April 29th carried a report of the battle stating, "The feds were mostly renegade Arkansians and desperate men. They fought well..." In his battle report General William L. Cabell himself gave a very great compliment to the Arkansas Federals: "The enemy all (both infantry and cavalry) fought well, equally as well as any Federal troops I have ever seen. Although it was thought by a great many that they would make but a feeble stand, the reverse, however, was the case, as they resisted every attack made on them, and, as fast driven out of one house, would occupy another and deliver their fire."[123]

Cabell retreated across the Boston Mountains and was unable to quickly pull his shattered forces back into battle readiness. Not knowing the desperation of the Confederate position, the Federals let their imaginations run away to conclusions of imminent Rebel attack.

Five days after the battle, Colonel Harrison wrote to General Curtis:

"Can we be re-enforced, and that immediately? We can never hold this place without artillery and horses. There is no use in disguising the fact. Last night I was positive that Cabell and the Fort Smith Indians had combined to attack me at daylight. My men stood under arms from midnight until after sunrise. Such an attack is brewing, and will come in force in a few days. We have no stores here; we have nothing to eat, and cannot get out trains, with good luck, until the 28th. Must we starve, and then have all the conscripts surrender to an overwhelming force, that will shoot them as deserters? We haul forage 45 miles, and weaken our command by large escorts. We can make no reconnaissances nor scouts for want of horses, and could not protect our rear and flanks in a retreat. The enemy are splendidly mounted. The men are brave, and have achieved a splendid victory, but we must have help or fall back. Answer immediately what I shall do...."[124]

And so, not surprisingly, the order came down from General Curtis for the Federal outpost at Fayetteville to be evacuated. Equipment, supplies and other items were loaded into wagons, and started out for Springfield, Missouri on the afternoon of April 24th, just six days after the successful battle to defend the town. The evacuation was completed by the following afternoon.

Union Dr. Carpenter was left in command of the hospital in town as the soldiers pulled out. For days no Confederates entered to take up the abandoned gift of Fayetteville that had been left to them. On May 1st, during the time between Union abandonment and Confederate occupation, the Fayetteville Female Seminary caught fire. It had been used as a hospital after the Battle of Prairie Grove. The women and children, who were about all that were left in town, formed a bucket brigade to battle the flames, and succeeded in saving the original log structure and part of the assembly room.

"At length, on the eleventh day" after the Battle of Fayetteville, Carpenter recorded, "a company of ragamuffins, under the command of one Capt. Palmer, who styled himself a 'Partisan Ranger,' appeared." There was justice and irony in this, for J.R. Palmer and his "ragamuffins" had been active participants in the battle on April 18th. Furthermore, Palmer was one and the same as the J.R. Palmer who was a dentist in Fayetteville prior to the war. He was occupying his home town.

The battle of Fayetteville had two interesting characteristics.

First, it was the quintessential Civil War battle, fought between Arkansas Confederates and Arkansas Unionists on Arkansas soil. Second, both sides can fairly claim to have won. Harrison won a tactical victory by repelling the attack and holding the town at the end of the battle. Yet Cabell won a strategic victory because the Federals decided they were too insecure to hold the post, and withdrew from Fayetteville on their own a week later. Both sides, then, can fairly claim their respective victories in the Battle of Fayetteville.

An Open Town

The Confederates did not stay in Fayetteville on a continuing basis. Rather, the town was wide open, subject to temporary occupation from any force that came by.

The summer of 1863 was filled with Confederate setbacks. On May 16th the Confederates were defeated at the battle of Champion Hill, Mississippi. Fayetteville's William O. Feemster, son of minister Mercus and Martha Feemster, was wounded and later died of his wounds. On July 3rd General Robert E. Lee and the Army of Northern Virginia were defeated at Gettysburg, Pennsylvania. James Parks, brother of Elizabeth Blakeley, was killed there.[125] The next day, much closer to home, the besieged city of Vicksburg on the Mississippi River fell. Also on the fourth, a Confederate assault on Helena failed to carry the town. On the ninth, Port Hudson, the last Rebel stronghold on the Mississippi River, surrendered. Numerous Arkansas regiments and thousands of Arkansas men were captured. The Confederacy was thereafter split in two, with Arkansas in what was called the Trans-Mississippi. On September 10th Union troops occupied Little Rock, compelling the Confederate state government to flee to Washington, Arkansas, where it remained for the duration of the war.

On August 22, 1863, Lt. Edward A. Barker of Company C of the 2nd Kansas Cavalry rode into Fayetteville at the head of a column of Federal soldiers. Only civilians were there so they went in unopposed and stayed the night. The next morning "we were reinforced by about 150 Mountain Federals under the command of Vanderpool and others," Barker reported.

One of these Union partisans was Lyman G. Bennett. "We...found the town, or what remained of it, in possession of sixty federal soldiers who had arrived the day before..." he wrote. "We were proceeding to the public square to go into camp when word was brought that Buck Brown, a noted bush ranger, was attacking the pickets."[126]

At that point, reported Lt. Barker, "the Mountain Federals fled in utter confusion. In the meantime, I made efforts to get my men together; ran into the stable to get my horse, and while there was captured by the rebels."[127] The skirmishing in town lasted about twenty minutes, when the Confederates withdrew with their prisoners.[128]

The people of Fayetteville lived with the knowledge that soldiers of either side may appear at any moment. "On the 31st of July the Feds dismounted our good neighbor Mrs. Nolen in the streets of Fayetteville, leaving her to foot it home and pack her saddle," recorded Robert Mecklin.[129]

During the summer of 1863 the civilian population of Fayetteville continued to decline. Retired educator Robert W. Mecklin wrote his sister about it. "Many citizens of this part of the state have gone North, the most of whom [we] are well rid of," he said, referring to people who not long ago had been his fellow educators and friends. These hard feelings were the price of civil war. Pastor Baxter had undergone the same transformation, but in the opposite direction. "But many others," Mecklin continued, "with whom we are loth to part, are running away South to save themselves from murder and their property from plunder. There are but few of us now left."[130]

The "property" Mecklin referred to was two fold in nature. Of course, one could not flee south to save his real estate. What he meant was animal stock like horses and cows, but more especially he meant slaves. It is interesting to note that some people would leave their lands, families and all other property and flee to Texas to save this one kind of property, their slaves. The farmer Joseph Lewis went south. Adeline Blakeley stated that "during the Civil War Mr. Parks took all his slaves and all of his fine stock, horses and cattle and went south to Louisiana following the Southern army for protection. Many slave owners left the county taking with them their slaves and followed the army."[131] Parks did not return until the war was over.

Seabe Tuttle, another slave in Washington County, described the same phenomenon. "Miss Mollie and Miss Nannie, and Miss Jim and another daughter...all went in carriages and wagons down south following the Confederate army. They took my pa, Mark, and other servants, my mother's sister, Americus and Barbary. They told them they would bring them back home after the war. Then my mother and me and the other darkies, men and women and children, followed them with the cattle and horses and food. But we didn't get no further than Dardanelle when the Federals captured us and took us back to the Federal garrison at Fort Smith, where they kept us six months."[132]

Judge David Walker, returned from seeing President Davis in Richmond, went to northwest Arkansas, and reported to Governor Flanagin. "I have just returned from the Mountain country," he wrote on June 9, 1863. "The spirit of resistance is stronger than ever, but it is, I fear, stimulated by revenge.... Those who have left their families and gone north, or who have relatives in the northern army, as well as some real or supposed sympathyzers with the old union, are robbed of all their valuable property. Indeed a pretty brisk business (in some places) is going on in stealing and plundering."[133] He was appointed as Colonel of Cavalry in the Confederate service, assigned as a member of military court of Lieutenant General Theophilus Holmes' Corp.[134]

Robert Mecklin in a letter dated August 9, 1863, described some of the contribution of the women of Fayetteville to the war. "We are still comfortably clad, though some of us may have to go barefoot next winter for want of leather and shoemakers," he said. This would indicate that the pre-war shoemakers Jacob Battenfield and John Ruth were gone. "Our women patch our old clothes and make us new ones, while themselves are comfortably and neatly dressed in garments of their own manufacture. The southern women left in this part of our state are seeing hard times but most of them bear the hardship with patience and fortitude. They will live in story, aye will they, till their grandchildren have reached their dotage. Some for their kindness and hospitality to the sick and wounded. Some for their skill and success in hiding their provisions to subsist on, and for concealing, feeding and aiding our weary way worn soldiers and their scouts; some for their lady like manners, which has saved their houses from plunder and themselves from insult; and still others for their dexterity in the use of the broomstick, poker and wash basin on Federal noggins.[135]

On September 8th Mecklin wrote to his sister that "[w]e have no doctor in the county, and very little medicine." This would identify more of the absent population of Fayetteville. The pre-war medical community was gone. These included the venerable Dr. Thomas Jefferson Pollard and his brother and fellow practitioner, Dr. Wade Pollard. Gone, too, were the young doctors, James Stevenson, George Taylor, Thomas Uncary, David Smithson and J. G. Scarborough. Of course, Dr. Bell had been killed at Wilson's Creek.

"It may be interesting to you," Mecklin wrote his sister, that "you will learn a few of the thousand difficulties with which we have to contend in getting along, the toils, cares, anxieties, confusion and stress both of body and mind which we suffer." Although he was an older man who stayed home throughout the entire war, he was in a sense one of its casualties. Everybody in Fayetteville was.

"We never see a newspaper," Mecklin continued. Most of the Negroes, he said, were gone. He found a neighbor woman "sewing up her sheets in which to hide away her wheat." He frequently heard shots in the distance. Federal soldiers would stop by now and again, and the Mecklins would hide their pony and other valuables. "The Federals have robbed Uncle Vince and Aunt Aggy of nearly everything they had."

Rumors were constantly circulating, frequently followed up by corrections, some of which were also inaccurate. Yet Mecklin was glad he stayed home. "I have fared perhaps as well or better than most of those who went south leaving their families behind," he said. "I have lost property but care little for it in comparison with the misery of being separated form my family. Some families have suffered much.... Oh when will this unholy war end! I do hope with the year 1863.... I do want peace and independence for the South."

Mecklin described in fascinating detail an encounter with Union soldiers while he was reading his Bible at home: "Well before I had finished reading those two chapters four Federals rode up to the gate on the north side of the house and seemed to hold a consultation, came up to the little gate north of wife's window and ask her sitting there if they could get some dinner. She said, 'We have but little and your chance for dinner poor.' They said, 'We want only milk and bread.' 'Get down then and walk round to the front door.' They did so and she met them in the parlor. They conducted themselves decently, at their (no, our) milk, bread, butter and syrup, returned to the parlor and had a low talk with wife, then left.

"When they first came in I laid down my Bible, went into the parlor with a police, 'How are you gentlemen,' took a squint at them, returned to wife's room, took up my Bible and turned over to the 12th chapter of Romans,[*] not to learn my duty as a warrior, but as a Christian. This is the way we get on. With an assumed cheerfulness to save ourselves from plunder and insult, we give away our bread...."[136]

Romans 12: 12-14: Rejoicing in hope, patient in tribulation, continuing instant in prayer, distributing to the necessity of saints, given to hospitality. Bless them which persecute you: bless and curse not.

The Return of Union Occupation

With the Union successes on every side, the question of whether to re-occupy Fayetteville came up among the Federal commanders. "I would also recommend the sending of Colonel Harrison's regiment (First Arkansas Cavalry)," General James G. Blunt wrote on September 13, 1863, to Major General James M. Schofield, "to occupy Northwestern Arkansas, with headquarters at Fayetteville. They understand the country thoroughly, and would be of great service in ridding that part of the country of guerillas, of which there are numerous bands in that locality. They could also protect the telegraph line, if it should be reconstructed."

Blunt's recommendation was quickly carried out. On Tuesday, September 22, 1863, the First Arkansas Union Cavalry marched back into Fayetteville. Some hearts were gladdened; others were not. "My ear was stunned by the hateful roar of Federal cannon in town," Mecklin complained, which was followed by "the shrill notes of the bugle struck up accompanied by the band playing some merry making...of a Yankee song in exultation at again having possession of Fayetteville."

The following month of October brought an increase in Confederate aggressiveness. On Sunday, October 11, 1863, at about 11:30 a.m. Confederate Captain Smithson of Brook's regiment brought in a flag of truce, bearing a message to Union Major Thomas Hunt: "To the Commander of the Federal Troops at Fayetteville: Sir: Having the town of Fayetteville surrounded by a superior force, and to prevent the effusion of blood, I demand the immediate surrender of the place and the troops within the same. Thirty minutes will be given for a reply. Very respectfully, W.H. Brooks, Colonel, Commanding."

There were Fayetteville citizens commanding both sides. Major Hunt answered by stating that "no surrender would me made without a fight."[137] Hunt formed his men in the town square, in line of battle, awaiting attack. When the assault did not occur, the men slept on their arms at camp. The square was strengthened with wagons and breastworks, with the intention that if an attack came the men would fall back to it as a final defense.

At 3 a.m. on October 12th the men were awakened to be ready in case of a daylight attack. It did not come, either then or any time that day. On the night of the 12th all wagons, military and civilian alike, were put into the Fayetteville public square for defense. There the men slept at their assigned posts. When morning dawned on the

13th, still no attack came.

Hunt estimated the Confederates that day to number upwards of one thousand, with Hunt himself commanding less than half that number. He estimated that his men would have less than full rations after two more days. "I am now making the best arrangements of the forces here," he wrote to General John McNeil, "in view of defending the place to the last." October 14th came and went. That night a hundred and fifty Union reenforcements rode in from Cassville. They reported that Brooks was gone, and the crisis was over.

About this time a guerrilla soldier by the name of Charles Hauptmann was captured by Union forces. In 1860 he had been a painter in Fayetteville. A check of the records showed that he was a paroled prisoner from an earlier capture, so he was sent to six months of hard labor for violating his oath.[138]

On October 29th one of the Union soldiers reenforcing the outpost wrote a letter home from Fayetteville. "Fayetteville is now a miserable dirty dreary looking place," said the soldier from the 18th Iowa. "The better part of the town is in ruins having been burned by the rebels last summer, the place being almost defenceless just before we came here... Fayetteville was once the first place in the Southwest for wealth, education, and refinement."[139]

Captain Joseph S, Robb's grave at the Fayetteville National Cemetery. Author's Collection.

In December one-time Fayetteville attorney Lafayette Gregg became colonel of the newly forming 4th Arkansas Union Cavalry in Little Rock. He led that regiment for the duration of the war. He was the highest ranking Federal soldiers from Fayetteville.

The year 1863 ended on a somber note for Colonel Marcus La Rue Harrison. One of his best officers was accidentally shot in the leg and he bled to death. On Christmas Eve an obviously distressed Harrison wrote to the departmental adjutant about it. "I would most respectfully report that Capt. Joseph S. Robb Co. L 1st Ark Cav died in hospital at this place at two o'clock a.m. 20th instant of accidental gunshot wound, ball passing between bones of the leg below the left knee cutting the main artery, causing excessive hemorrhage," he wrote. Turning reflective, he added, "Very little is known of his relations except that his mother is a Mrs. Cynthia House of Palmyra, Iowa. Capt. Robb was a very gallant officer and tendered much important service to this government.... I believe him to have been thoroughly honest." [140] Captain Robb's grave is in the Fayetteville National Cemetery.

1864
An Occupied Town in an Endless War

"The business of killing men still goes bravely on."

      Fayetteville was always under Union control from September 1863 until the end of the war. A large percentage of the people in town were Federal soldiers of the First Arkansas Union Cavalry. The local population was severely depleted, consisting mostly of women and children who lived the life of civilians in a militarily occupied town. Many who remained were probably glad for the Federal presence and supported it, but others resented it and worked quietly against it. For example, Martha Van Hoose once smuggled boots for a Confederate officer through town under her hooped skirt.

Colonel Marcus LaRue Harrison. Washington County Historical Society.

      There was no civil government of any kind. This made the military post commander, Colonel M. LaRue Harrison, the most important person in town for both soldiers and civilians. All things considered, his rule of Fayetteville was a mild one. Unlike many Northerners, he liked Arkansas and its people. His nature was not naturally harsh, and he restrained the anger of others. During the war he, along with some other Union soldiers, joined the Masonic lodge, which met at the lone public building which was not destroyed. The discipline he maintained among the soldiers was temperate. Yet it must also be said that he was a post commander in the midst of war, and his actions were not always perfect and not everyone liked him. On balance, Fayetteville was fortunate to have such a man of moderation in war time.

A rumor arose that in view of the increasing number of Federal regiments formed and yet forming in Arkansas, that a Brigadier General was to be appointed from the state. In a letter to General Samuel Curtis, Colonel Harrison made it known that he was the senior commander of the Arkansas regiments and that he desired the position. After stating that he had voted for Curtis back in Iowa when Curtis ran for Congress, Harrison stated that "I claim to be an Arkansian because I espoused her cause in the darkest hour," This was truly said. His statement that he intended "to make that state my home at the close of the war" was not a mere self-serving assertion; that is precisely what he later did. Harrison was the chief architect of Arkansas troops being permitted to serve in the Union Army under their own state banner, and he was then and is now entitled to the credit for it. But there was no Arkansas brigadier general appointed, and Harrison remained on the with the regiment as its Colonel. At the very end of the war, after peace had been concluded, Harrison was promoted, along with many others across the Union Army, to the brevet (or temporary) rank of Brigadier General as a gesture of courtesy.[141]

A little adventure on Christmas Eve of 1863 was one of the first things Colonel Harrison had to deal with in 1864. He himself drew up the charges against Second Lieutenant Jacob H. Keiser of Company D. The first charge was "conduct unbecoming an officer and a gentleman," the specification of which was that Keiser "did black his face and dress himself in womens clothes and did proceed, thus disguised, to the store of one W. [Washington] L. Wilson, a merchant of Fayetteville, Arkansas, and did enter said store in search of goods." The second charge of "attempting larceny" was that Keiser "did proceed at the head of a squad of enlisted men... and did forcibly enter the store... in search of goods." It was not long before Lt. Keiser was dismissed from the Army. It appears from this episode that Wilson was, at least to some extent, back in business at this time.[142]

From its headquarters in Fayetteville, the Federal campaign against the Rebel guerrillas in northwest Arkansas was pursued to the limit of endurance of both men and horses. The Arkansas men who were raised in the area were the best weapon the Union Army had against guerrillas. "They are already doing good service as Scouts," wrote Sergeant Charles O. Musser of the 29th Iowa concerning the Arkansas Unionists. "They are acquainted with the country and Know who are loyal and who are not."[143] Yet the essential fact remained true: neither the Union nor the Confederacy would commit enough men and resources to Arkansas to win the war there. The year of 1864 was characterized by long hard scout patrols involving brief and sometimes deadly skrimishes. Robert Mecklin noted in his letter on February 4 1864, that "the business of killing men still goes bravely on. Scarcely a day passes during which we do not hear of one or more bushwhackers being killed or that some Federals have been killed by them."

Hard riding scouting expeditions were continually going out of an returning to town. Company M of the First Arkansas Union Cavalry had a particularly active writer of company returns during 1864 to chronicle this activity. At the end of February he reported on the first two months of the war:

This shadowy photograph is believed to be of the First Arkansas Union Light Artillery, recruited and based in Fayetteville. It is the best Civil War image from northwest Arkansas. Washington County Historical Society.

"Jany. 18. Lt. Roseman started on a scout to Searcy Co, Ark with twenty of the Company, they were in two engagements... in which the revels were defeated with loss - the men were out until Feby. 24, and participated in several skirmishes and were constantly on scouting duty - over 100 rebels were killed on the trip.* Feby. 25 Lt. Roseman again went out with 33 men remaining till 29th, the company killed four rebels on the trip. Various other detachments of the Company have been in scouts other than those named. In an engagement on the White River Washington Co. Ark Private John K. Johnson was killed. Since last muster the Company has been constantly scouting. Quite a number of horses have been killed, abandoned, etc. - and a number captured. The Company is in a good scouoting condition considering the great scarcity of forage."

The April 1864 return of Company M continued the same story: "Mch 3rd Lt. Roseman took 38 of the Company and proceeded on a five days scout in which three rebels were killed and Pvt John Hunter was wounded. He returned on the 7th. On the 9th Lt. Roseman took 48 of the Company and went on a scout returning on the 12th. On the 13th he took 35 of Company on scout with paymaster to Neosho Mo, returning on the 18th. On the 19th Lt. Roseman with 30 of the Company proceeded to escort Stark's battery from Fayetteville to Ft. Smith. He returned the 24th. Mch. 27th the Co. Moved from Fayetteville to Clarksville reaching the latter place 31st. Distance traveled during the month 527 miles."[144]

In February Union Major General Samuel R. Curtis went on an extended tour of his military domain called the Department of Kansas. One can easily imagine the prepatory work of cleaning and making things orderly by Harrison's men in Fayetteville ahead of the general's arrival. In reporting to Washington, D.C., of his findings, Curtis stated that "Fayetteville is a high place, easily defended, but much exposed, being very remote from other posts. The troops (First Arkansas Cavalry) are much scattered." Five days later Curtis sent a letter to the Department of Missouri saying, "On this [north] side of the Arkansas [River] small bands [of Rebels] from 3 to 50 are occasionally found; several such bands are near Fayetteville, Ark., where the First Arkansas Cavalry holds a very loose and scattered command."

The residents of Fayetteville, whether in town, in the military, or in places of refuge, tried to keep each other apprised by letter of what was happening to family and friends. The mails were inconsistent and many messages sent were never received. In a letter dated September 11, 1864, Isaac Henry of Brooks' regiment wrote a letter to his wife, Catherine, who lived two miles north of Fayetteville.

---

* *This number of 100 casualties is most unlikely.*

"I... want sister Louisa to write," he said, "and to write all the news, and write who is died and killed and who has gone north and what has become of everybody in general as we cant get any news from that country."[145]

From his fugitive home in Camden, Arkansas, Judge, now Colonel, David Walker wrote on February 10th to his son-in-law, James D. Walker, who was once of Fayetteville and now in Texas. "Mr. Lewis' negro women all went off taking with them a good bed and clothing for each of them. Mr. Feemster's family had been sick," he wrote. "The country is being wasted away and soon will be a wide wild waste.... Doctor Stevenson left here this morning for Kentucky."

The transformation from civilian to soldier can be seen in the face of Captain Wythe Walker of the 34th Arkansas Confederate Infantry. Washington County Historical Society.

In another letter to his son-in-law dated August 23, 1864, Judge Walker passed on the latest news from home. "Mr. Purdy is just in from Fayetteville, was wounded and confined there for a month or two. He says Mr. Pegram was compelled to leave his family and go to Springfield to save his life.... Mr. Carnahan's family were well, so was Mr. Freyschlag's and Aunt Jane. Ned was with Brown. Alf Wilson's house was burned. Mrs. Gunter saved part of her household effects."[146]

Judge Walker had long since come full circle on his political feelings. Starting as a strong supporter of the Union, he made the leap to the Confederate cause because he, like most Southerners, loved his state more than his nation. His state was, in fact, his nation, which had always been the prevailing sentiment in the South. From there he developed an intense Southern patriotism that took him whole heartedly into support of the war effort. This support could not be shaken even by the catastrophe that had befallen his family, Fayetteville, and Arkansas. "I sit and think over this horrid war and all its blighting affects, our situation, past, present and prospective," he wrote in January 1864. "I can compare it to nothing imaginable save the coming of the flood which God in his wrath sent to scourge a sinful and rebellious world."[147]

On February 29th Judge Walker addressed a portion of a letter to his grandson, David Walker. The determination the Confederates to succeed, and to sacrifice their family in pursuit of that success, is remarkably evident in this message. "This is your last year at school until the war is over," the grandfather wrote. "After this year your country will call you to fill a brother's place or stand by a brother's side - and if I live I too will be near you in the hour of deadly conflict."[148] The transformation from peace to war had wrought such changes in feelings.

The war was hard on everyone. The people at home worried about the soldiers who had gone off to war, and the soldiers worried about their families back home. Washington County Clerk Presley Smith was one of the few Confederate sympathizers to remain in Fayetteville throughout the war. Governmental functions were suspended after 1861, so he had no official work to perform. Yet he rendered a great service to the people by his foresight in taking the county records and hiding them in Fincher's Cave. The records were there when the courthouse was burned, thus being saved for posterity. During the course of the war years his wife, Mary, died. His daughter-in-law, Lucretia Smith, the former head of the Fayetteville Female Academy, also passed away during the war although she was only in her mid-thirties. Lafayette and Mary Gregg had a daughter born on the last day of 1863. To their children Alfred and Andrew they now added Alice. She died on August 26, 1864.

Marshall Henry, who lived on the north end of town, told of the soldier's concern for his family at home. "My friends," he wrote on August 24, 1864, "I am very uneasy about you. I fear that you are suffering for something to eat....if it were so that I could be any help to you by going home I would start in the morning but I know that I could be no advantage at all but a disadvantage so will have to reconcile myself to stay where I am at present.... If you have any Confederate money on hand you had better let it off for it will be dead the first of January.... Tell all the girls that if I live till peace is made that I am a candidate for matrimony and that I am coming to old Washington County for I think the best women in the world lives in Washington County.... I want you all to remember me in your prayers to God. Pray God to preserve and protect me during this cruel war. O may God preserve and protect us all is my prayer."[149]

    The fighting continued. On April 30th was the Battle of Jenkin's Ferry southwest of Little Rock. Fayetteville's 34th Arkansas was in the thick of it. John Wilson was killed. Colonel William Brooks and Lieutenant Colonel James R. Pettigrew were wounded, though they later recovered and returned to active duty. Captain Jacob Wythe Walker was also wounded. His father, Judge David Walker, went to him and nursed him as best he could for weeks, but he could not be saved. "A good and pure and noble boy," the grieving father wrote in a notebook. "A most loving and obedient son... Like all persons of true merit, gentle and forgiving. Highly intellectual... The pride of a father."[150] The bullet that brought him down cared nothing for such virtues.

    When William Quesenberry, who was in Texas, heard of Wythe Walker's death, he sent a letter of consolation to Judge Walker. "I have just heard of the death of Wythe," he wrote on May 9th. "There was not a human being whom I esteemed more. I loved him as well as if he had been my own blood. Never did I more fully realize the horror of war than when I heard he had gone down upon the battle field. I do not offer you condolence...the whole world could give you no consolation. Your first-born struck down- the one perhaps you had a tenderer affection for than any other of your children - the child that linked you to your young days when you were happy in your hopes of the future - a thousand associations cannot but weigh upon you and cause you to feel the full meaning of that dark word - sorrow."[151]

    An important tool in the Federal war in northwest Arkansas was the loyalty oath, which was a simple affirmation of loyalty to the United States. One needed to say it, or to write it, in order to pass through Union lines, or draw supplies, or transact business. It was the bane of Confederate sympathizers, who detested it with all their hearts.

    Fayetteville post commander Colonel Harrison waged a

relentless war on Rebel-held areas by driving out anyone who would not take an oath of allegiance to the United States. In the summer of 1864 he launched an effort to re-structure northwest Arkansas society with a new and more stringent requirement. The oath became a vehicle by which freedoms, supplies, and other benefits would be dispensed or withheld.

On June 16, 1864, the following order was issued:

"I. All citizens of this place, male or female, who have not yet taken the Oath of Allegiance to the United States Government, and who shall fail to do the same before the 23d inst., will be sent beyond the limits of this command, except the two following classes: viz., married women, whose husbands are known to be loyal, and children who are minors.

"II. Ladies, whose husbands or natural protectors are in the service of the enemy north of the Arkansas River, will be sent beyond the lines.

"III. Transportation to Fort Smith will be furnished to such as do not desire, or are not allowed by the terms of Paragraph II, to take the oath of Allegiance."

The citizens of Fayetteville had the choice to either take the oath or leave. People consulted their hearts and consciences and made their decisions.

Mary Stone. Shiloh Museum.

"I, Mary Stone, of the County of Washington, State of Arkansas," wrote a Fayetteville young woman on the pre-printed oath form, "do solemnly swear, in the presence of Almighty God, that I will henceforth faithfully support, protect and defend the Constitution of the United States, and the Union of the States thereunder, and that I will in like manner abide by and faithfully support all acts of Congress passed during the existing rebellion, with reference to slaves..., and that I will in like manner abide by and faithfully support all proclamations of the President made during the existing rebellion, having reference to slaves... so help me God." It was endorsed "subscribed and sworn to before me, at Fayetteville, Ark., this 20 day of June, 1864," and signed by the provost marshal.[152]

Mary Stone was the last graduate of the Female Female Seminary in 1861. In 1864 she was twenty years old and living with her family. Her father, Stephen K. Stone, had lost his mercantile business in the flames of 1862. They had once owned seven slaves, who were by then long since free. Now, she had to swear allegiance to the Union and support emancipation, or leave her home. She bowed to what probably seemed to her like the inevitable future, took the oath, and stayed home.

After the commissioning as Colonel of a new Federal regiment, the Fourth Arkansas Union Cavalry, Fayetteville attorney Lafayette Gregg spent most of the year 1864 in Little Rock organizing his command. He led that regiment for the duration of the war. No other Fayetteville men are known to have gone into that unit.

Fayetteville was occupied throughout the entire year of 1864 by the First Arkansas Union Cavalry. Two disciplinary actions within the regiment involved men from the Fayetteville area. First Lieutenant Thomas Wilhite and Captain Jesse M. Gilstrap were early Washington County men in the Federal service. Both were successful recruiters for the regiment, and both known for their personal courage. Yet both were ordered dishonorably dismissed from the service of the United States.

Lt. Wilhite was clearly a favorite

Fayetteville attorney Lafayette Gregg became the Colonel and commander of the Fourth Arkansas Union Cavalry. He was the highest ranking Federal officer from Fayetteville. Gregg Family Papers (MC 1000), Box 3-7, photograph no. 1, Special Collections, University of Arkansas Libraries, Fayetteville.

of Lt. Col. Bishop, who devoted a chapter to his life in his 1863 book, *Loyalty on the Frontier*.[153] His Unionist defiance in the face of "secession fever" earned the admiration of many. The record is scant as to the offending conduct, but it involved some manifestation of "incompetency," which was given as the cause of his discharge.

Lieutenant Thomas Wilhite. Prairie Grove Battlefield State Park.

Wilhite's friends did not forget him in his hour of need. While his dishonorable discharge was pending, a number of officers got together and petitioned Major General James M. Schofield for a reprieve. "Lt Wilhite was one of the first men of Arkansas who took a positive and determined stand for the Union," they wrote. "He was active and zealous in his efforts to fill the 1st Ark Cav and but few men have contributed more towards the raising of the Regiment than himself.... He does not claim to be an educated officer, is distrustful of his executive ability as Commander of a Company, and has already once waived his claim to that position...in favor of an officer of another company.... He is now absent in comd of scouting party and has no knowledge whatever of the preferring of this request." The request did fall upon deaf ears. The pending order of dishonorable discharge of Thomas Wilhite was modified so as to reflect an honorable resignation.[154]

Captain Jesse Gilstrap was a similar case. He was one of the early enlistees from Arkansas, and upon the organization of the regiment was installed as Captain of Company D in July 1862. After a year and a half of service he was put out of the Army for "failing to make proper company returns since his appointment," "lax discipline permitting his men to be disrespectful to him," "sleeping out of his quarters without leave," and "uncleanliness of person to a degree totally unbecoming his position."

Gilstrap petitioned that he be permitted to be honorably discharged. In a detailed letter to Major General Rosecrans, he reviewed his military service and contribution to the cause of the Union. He admitted his failure to make proper returns in a timely fashion, but denied all other accusations. The letter was signed by Major Hunt, six captains and several lieutenants of the Regiment along with the surgeon and assistant surgeon. Notably absent was the signature of Colonel Harrison. The petition for an honorable release was granted.[155]

Absenteeism of the Federal troops in Fayetteville was nearly an epidemic. After all, these were mostly Arkansas men stationed near their own homes. A considerable percentage of the enlisted men were at one time or another absent without leave (AWOL). Colonel William A. Phillips, who commanded the district in which Fayetteville was located, wrote to General Curtis about the First Arkansas in March 1863 that "I visited and reviewed the Arkansas troops three days ago. I was, in the main, pleased with their appearance, but the disposition to go home is too general, and I found it necessary to check it. This has given me a good deal of trouble in the Indian command, but I find the Arkansas command worse than they are."[156]

Union General John McNeil, the commander of the District of Southwest Missouri, lost his temper over absenteeism in the First Arkansas. On August 6th he sent out two orders specifically to the regiment. First, "all enlisted men of your Regiment absent without leave [are to] be reported as deserters, and, if apprehended, they will be treated as such." The second order stated that "no more furloughs will be approved.... The number of enlisted men of your regiment, absent on furlough, already exceeds five per centum of the whole number present for duty."

Thomas J. Hunt.
Author's Collection.

An interesting but not surprising development of the occupation of Fayetteville by Union troops was the unavoidable contact between young soldiers and the local young women. Union Major Thomas J. Hunt grew up soouth of town and lived his entire life in Arkansas. His father, William Hunt, was the veterinarian surgeon for the First Arkansas Cavalry. It is interesting that during the war Tom

Hunt changed jobs from teacher to soldier, stayed at home for both careers, married Matilda Campbell on May 29, 1863, and had two daughters (Nora, born February 27, 1864, and Virginia, born August 18, 1865). This was indeed an unusual Civil War military career.

Thursday, April 7, 1864, was one of the deadliest day of the war for the First Arkansas Union Cavalry. The unlikely scenario for this was that of nine men assigned to guard regimental corrals southwest of Fayetteville not far from the old battlefield of Prairie Grove. During the evening about twenty guerillas under one Lyon struck, killing/executing all nine Federal soldiers.

In October Rebel guerrillas under Buck Brown and soldiers under Colonel William Brooks began an encirclement of Fayetteville. On October 27th the shooting began. "Fayetteville was attacked this morning by a strong force, who posted themselves at sunrise on the almost inaccessible bluffs of East Mountain, about 1,000 yards east of town, and opened a brisk fire on my camp," Colonel Harrison reported to his superiors. "I immediately ordered Capt. D.C. Hopkins, supported by Capt. E.B. Harrison, to move up the mountain with a line of idsmounted skirmishers. When within about 200 yards of the top of the bluff they engaged the enemy, who, as soon as theor exact position was ascertained, I commenced shelling with a 12-pounder mountain howitzer, causing them to move their position several times. Atthe same time, Captain Hopkins and Captain Harrison led their men, less than 100 strong, up the mountain in the face of a galling fire from 700 rebels, charging the topmost bluff three times, and the third time driving the enemy from their position."[157]

The Confederates did not leave the area, however, and Fayetteville was essentilly under siege. Food rations were drastically cut. By sunlight in the day and by torchlight at night, Captain Hugo Boteufhr directed the construction of improvements upon the town fortifications. Further attach could come at any time, and the First Arkansas prepared for it daily.

When the regular Confederate cavalry retreated into northwest Arkansas after their unsuccessful raid with General Sterling Price through Missouri, Major General James F. Fagan was detached and sent southward by way of Fayetteville. There, on the morning of November 3, 1864, hostilities commenced again.

Harrison described the situation: "They attacked my pickets and commenced bombarding the town with all their boasted chivalry, not giving me the least time to remove families (most of their own at that) nor demanding a surrender. The bombardment was kept up with one 6-pounder rifled gun and one 12-pounder field howitzer until nearly sunset. Three times the order was given to charge the works, but each time the men on coming within range of my rifles shrank from the assault and fled to a safe position. At sunset the retreat of the enemy commenced and was continued during the whole night....at sunrise on the 4th instant only about 600 remained to cover the retreat.... My loss was 9 wounded - 1 mortally, 8 slightly. The strength of my command during the engagement was 958 volunteers and 170 militia...."

It was doubtful that the Confederates ever had any serious intentions of taking Fayetteville in this attack, which is sometimes denoted as "the second battle of Fayetteville." Certainly the casualties are not indicative of a strong intent. With their numerical superiority at the time of Fagan's arrival, they could have taken the place had they really wanted it. Unfortunately, there are no reports on the incident from Brown, Brooks or Fagan, and one can only speculate at what was really going on. Fagan was most likely just making a demonstration against Fayetteville while working his way south from the Missouri campaign. With a Union army in pursuit, the town would only have to be defended if taken. Fagan was gone on the morning of the 4th, and the following day Federal reinforcements arrived and the siege was over.

Toward the end of the year Colonel Harrison commented on the arduous task of scouting northwest Arkansas. "The duties devolving upon my command (eleven companies of cavalry)," Harrison wrote on November 10, 1864, "which was the only one in a country 110 miles broad and 250 miles long, have been so arduous that with from 100 to 300 horses (the greatest number at any one time on hand during the summer and autumn) it has been impossible to carry mails..., keep the telegraph in repair, forage for the post, escort supply trains, and at the same time to do the amount of scouting necessary to keep the country rid of the roving bands of the enemy."

The people of Fayetteville could not participate in the presidential election of 1864. As a seceded state, there was no presidential voting allowed in Arkansas. Still, there was interest. Abraham Lincoln was the Republican candidate for re-election, and was opposed by his one-time commanding general, George McClellan. Although he repudiated the Democratic peace platform upon which the party nominated him, McClellan was nonetheless essentially a peace candidate.

John Bowen of the Fayetteville area on October 1st wrote a letter about the election. "Dear Brother and Sister.... We have but little news heare," he reported. "The[re] is some excitement heare about the election they appear to be divide some for Linkern and some for McClellan.... times is very dul i heare money is scarse.... Some thinks that if McClellan is elected President that peace wood be made in a short time but we cannot tell wether it would so or not If he would bring a short pease I would be glad if he was elected." McClellan was not elected, however, and Lincoln carried the war on toward its conclusion.

Private W.C. Peerson of Company B wrote a brief description of his service as a ordinary soldier in the First Arkansas Union Cavalry on January 12, 1865. "We have had a very hard time since we have been stationed at this Post [Fayetteville]. Had a great deal of hard fighting to do. We have been surrounded for days that we darsen to show oourselves outside the Post. I have been in more than a dozen hard fights with the Rebels since I have been in service, Have had two horses shot from under me by the Rebels though I have had the good luck to not get wounded myself, although I have had several balls shot through my clothes. I have at this time 9 months to serve before my time is out and I sincerely hope that I may have as good luck for the rest of my time.... And if I should live through and get my discharge, I shall feel that I have done my part for my country. If every man in the Army had done as much as I have already done, this cruel war would be over."[158]

The year of 1864 ended essentially as it had begun. An entire year of death, sacrifice and deprivation had accomplished nothing. Twelve hard months had no materially advanced the cause of either side. By comparison to years earlier, nothing much happened in 1864. Secession had already occurred. The regiments had already been recruited and the men and boys had marched away. The town had already been destroyed. The people, which and black, were already mostly gone. Those that remained just carried on, enduring, hoping that somehow this long nightmare would end. But it did not end. It was a hard year in which hopes for peace were dashed and the war went on endlessly.

1865
Peace from the East

"All is now peace and tranquility here... I could not have believed that such a change could have taken place so soon."

As the new year of 1865 began in Fayetteville, it was not known that the end of the war was nearly at hand. Although the struggle for Southern independence was not going well, nothing of any real significance had happened in Arkansas in all of 1864. Another year of war seemed to be in the offing.

On January 10th Judge Walker was in the town of Washington, Arkansas, the Confederate capital after the fall of Little Rock. "Gen. Price has gone on a visit to his family in Texas," he wrote in a letter. "We have no apprehension of an advance of the enemy this winter; perhaps next spring some move will be made upon us."[159] False rumors boosted morale. In a letter from a friend dated January 25th, Walker was told that "The new year has brought s more cheering political news - in bona fide foreign intervention, and our recognition after a certain time as a separate nationality, in which Mr. Lincoln has no part or sway."[160]

Fayetteville remained under Union control because there were large numbers of Federal soldiers continually there, but the surrounding countryside held by the Rebels. Union control went where Federal soldiers went and no further. During this year," Lt. Col. Bishop wrote of 1865, "a relentless warfare was carried on against the small band of guerillas who infested northwestern Arkansas, and many were killed." This was indeed so, for although the war was slowly moving to a foreseeable conclusion in the eastern part of the Confederacy, it continued unabated in the West without prospect for an end. The truth of it was the war could not be won by the Union Army in northwest Arkansas. The vastness of wild hills and mountains, the innumerable valleys and caves, and the unwillingness of so many of the people to submit to Federal authority rendered the task of military conquest virtually impossible. Neither the Union nor the Confederacy could commit the men and resources necessary to win the war in Arkansas. If peace was to come, it would have to come from the East.

On January 24th there was a sharp fight near Fayetteville. Three Union soldiers were killed. On Marcgh 12th Federal Major John L. Worthington was killed "at the head of his men while leading a charge against a column of bushwhackers." Just two days later, the Confederates lost one of their most prominent leaders, guerrilla leader William "Buck" Brown. There many other brief engagements throughout the area.

James and Melinda McIlroy Van Hoose. Like several other young Fayetteville women, she died during the war. Shiloh Museum.

Like every other family in Fayetteville, the Van Hoose clan was shattered by the war. George Van Hoose was a Confederate prisoner on Johnson's Island in Ohio. Peter was a prisoner in Springfield, Missouri, and Elizabeth had married and gone south to teach school. Melinda McIlroy Van Hoose died at the age of twenty-eight in the fall of 1864. Her husband, James, went to visit his brother, Peter. There the two men received a letter from George, who said he did not think he could survive another winter in the harsh conditions of prison.

James Van Hoose secured various letters of recommendation from Union people in Arkansas and Missorui and went to Washington, D.C., to get permission to visit George on Johnson's Island. Secretary of War Edwin M. Stanton brushed him off and said only the President could grant such a request. On a day when President Lincoln was receiving public visitors, Van Hoose got at the end of a long line that was working its way to the Commander in Chief. However, when he got there he found himself speechless and only shook hands with the President.

Undeterred, he returned a couple of days later and was introduced to the President by Senator Lazarus W. Powell of Kentucky. When Van Hoose requested permission to visit his brother in prison, Lincoln refused. Van Hoose persisted and the President relented, writing out a permission in longhand, signed with the usual, "A. Lincoln." At the end of the conversation they shook hands again. It was February 1865, and Lincoln had but a few weeks to live.

Although it was not clear that surrender was so near, it was very apparent to the people of the South that the Confederacy was nowhere near victory. Determination and hope were strong among many Confederates, but overwhelming numbers of men, cannons, muskets and munitions were arrayed against them. No one knew what surrender would bring. Would all the Southern soldiers be sent to prisons in the North? Would the leaders be executed as traitors? What rights, if any, would Southern citizens have after the war? Would their lands be confiscated and given to the ex-slaves?

David Walker, once a strong Unionist, held out hope for Southern victory to the end. Shiloh Museum.

David Walker, the 1861 Unionist delegate from Fayetteville, was still a die-hard Rebel in 1865. "My opinion is that we will not surrender," he wrote optimistically on May 6th. Maybe he was trying to convince himself. "I should regret if such were the case. When our men lay down their arms, we may expect no mercy. They will hold the rebel states as conquered territories and claim all the spoils of victory."[161] This man who loved the Union and sought to preserve it in 1861, became a determined Confederate. As it came to be perceived that the war was lost, his shift in opinion was sharp. "I cannot think for a moment with any degree of patience upon reunion or if you please, subjugation, for the one necessarily comes with the other... I shudder at the thought of giving up our arms and being placed at the mercy of an infuriated merciless enemy. You know that I went into this war reluctantly, but under the circumstances felt a necessary duty, but entered it without mental reservation, with a will to see it out to the end."[162] This was truly said.

Even the able and revered General Robert E. Lee in far away Virginia could no longer hold bac the blue tide overwhelming the South. On April 2, 1865, his lines gave way and the Confederate capital of Richmond fell to Union forces. Lee withdrew his army westward but was caught in a vise from which he could not escape. There was no longer a point in resisting, and he surrendered the Army of Northern Virginia a week later in Appomattox Court House.

Although Lee's surrender was a severe blow to the South, it was not clear that the war was actually and fully over. President Jefferson Davis was in flight southward with some of his Cabinet members and generals, and he was wanting to go to Texas and fight on for Confederate independence.

General Joseph Johnston, commander of the largest remaining Rebel army, did not agree. He thought that the war was lost and it was time to end the killing. He surrendered is Army of Tennessee on April 26th in North Carolina. Following in turn, General Richard Taylor on May 4th surrendered the Department of Alabama, Mississippi and East Louisiana. This involved many regiments and soldiers from Arkansas and Fayetteville.

A month after Lee's surrender, Arkansas was still in a war zone. General E. Kirby Smith who commanded west of the Mississippi River began planning to continue the war as Jefferson Davis had hoped to do. As he traveled through Texas to rally his troops, his wiser subordinate, General Simon B. Buckner, surrendered the Department of the Trans-Mississippi in New Orleans on May 26th.

The Civil War in Fayetteville, Arkansas, was over. It had been an unmitigated catastrophe. The town itself was in ruins. The schools, the businesses, the courthouse and many homes, were burned. What had been built up for thirty years was mostly demolished. The economy was shattered. The people were scattered, many never to return.

The destroyed town of Fayetteville had to start over. Homes for the people had to be repaired and new ones made. Businesses had to be re-built and goods offered for sale. Farmers needed to plant crops. Public buildings had to be constructed again. Schools had to be founded and staffed with teachers. Churches needed to be reorganized and ministers brought in. Most of all, the citizens of Fayetteville needed to come home. The good people who had been there just five years ago in 1860, whether they had been Confederates or Unionists, needed to again become one, working together for the common benefit. Mutual confidence and trust among the citizens had to be re-established.

Many of the people did come home. Despite all the evils of civil war, they found a way to live with each other and move into the future. Fayetteville, it turned out, was not ending. It was only beginning again.

THE END.

Endnotes

1. Marian Tebbetts Banes, *The Journal of Marian Tebbetts Banes* (Fayetteville: Washington County Historical Society, undated), p. 59.

2. *The Fayetteville Daily Democrat*, July 3, 1928, p. 7.

3. No Author Stated, *History of Washington County Arkansas* (Springdale, Arkansas: Shiloh Museum, 1989), p. 156.

4. Waterman L. Ormsby, *The Butterfield Overland Mail* (San Marino, California: The Huntington Library, 1954), p. 19.

5. William S. Campbell, *One Hundred Years of Fayetteville, 1828-1928* (Fayetteville: Republished by the Washington County Historical Society, 1977), p. 19.

6. Campbell, p. 24.

7. The 1860 United States census for Fayetteville, Washington County, Arkansas.

8. Jason G. Gauthier, *Measuring America: The Decennial Censuses from 1790 to 2000* (Washington, D.C.: U.S. Census Bureau, 2002). p. 9.

9. No Author Stated, *History of Benton, Washington, Carroll, Madison, Crawford, Franklin and Sebastian Counties, Arkansas* (Chicago: The Goodspeed Publishing Company, 1889), pp. 234-235.

10. William Furry, Ed., *The Preacher's Tale: The Civil War Journal of Rev. Francis Springer* (Fayetteville: The University of Arkansas Press, 2001), pp. 32-33.

11. W. T. Moore, Ed., *The Living Pulpit of the Christian Church* (Cincinatti: R.W. Carroll and Co., 1868), p. 430.

12. Banes, p. 77.

13. Narnee Murphy, "Fayetteville's Earliest Methodist Church," *Flashback* (A publication of the Washington County Historical Society, Vol 43 #3, August 1993), p. 46

14. Campbell, pp. 12-13.

15. No Author Stated, *Union List of Arkansas Newspapers, 1819-1942* (Little Rock: Historical Records Survey of the Works

Project Administration), p. 44.

16. Goodspeed p. 244.

17. Campbell, p. 107.

18. Campbell, p. 107.

19. Campbell, pp. 11, 38.

20. Banes, pp. 47-48.

21. Campbell, p. 11.

22. Banes, p. 49.

23. Goodspeed, pp. 201-202.

24. Barbara Easley and Verla McAnelly, Ed., *Obituaries of Washington County, Arkansas, Volume I, 1841-1892* (Bowie, Maryland: Heritage Books, Inc., 1996), p. 209.

25. Goodspeed, pp. 200-201.

26. Ted R. Worley, "The Story of Alfred W. Arrington," *Arkansas Historical Quarterly*, Vol 14 #4, Winter 1955, pp. 315-339.

27. W. J. Lemke, Ed., *The Walker Family Album* (Fayetteville: Washington County Historical Society, 1964), unpaginated.

28. Banes, p. 81.

29. Campbell, pp. 34-35.

30. Banes, p. 59.

31. No Author Stated, History of Washington County Arkansas, p. 150.

32. *Flashback*, Vol 5 #5 Oct 1955 pp. 33-35.

33. Easley & McAnelly, pp. 16-24.

34. Orville W. Taylor, *Negro Slavery in Arkansas*, (Durham, N.C.: Duke University Press, 1958), pp. 112-113.

35. Banes, pp. 75-76.

36. Interview of Adeline Blakely. *Born in Slavery: Slave Narratives from the Federal Writers' Project, 1936-1938*. Arkansas Narratives, Volume II, Part I, p. 15. Interview by Zillah Cross Pell, pp. 11-16.

Interview by Mary D. Hudgins, pp. 180-193. P. 182.

37. Adeline Blakely Slave Narrative, pp. 11-16.

38. Roman J. Zorn, "An Arkansas Slave Incident and Its International Repercussions," *Arkansas Historical Quarterly*, Vol XVI #2, Summer 1957, pp. 139-149.

39. No Author Stated, *History of Washington County Ark.,* p. 161.

40. Banes, p. 59.

41. Adeline Blakely Slave Narrative, p. 12.

42. Campbell, p. 26.

43. Fayetteville Public Library, Wilson Family Papers.

44. Fayetteville Public Library, Van Hoose Family Papers.

45. Fayetteville Public Library, Van Hoose Papers, *Fayetteville Weekly Democrat,* June 28, 1894.

46. Goodspeed, p. 172.

47. Jack B. Scroggs, "Arkansas in the Secession Crisis," *Arkansas Historical Quarterly*, Vol 12 #3, Autumn 1953, p. 191.

48. Lemke, *Walker Family Letters*, no pagination.

49. Lemke, *Walker Family Letters*, no pagination.

50. *Flashback*, Vol. 47, #1, Feb. 1997 p 39.

51. Goodspeed, pp. 204-205.

52. Fayetteville Public Library, Van Hoose Family Papers.

53. Fayetteville Public Library, Wilson Family Papers.

54. W. J. Lemke, *The Life and Letters of Judge David Walker* (Fayetteville: Washington County Historical Society, 1957), p. 45.

55. Goodspeed, p. 205.

56. Campbell, p. 44.

57. Lemke, *The Life and Letters of Judge David Walker*, p. 44.

58. The Avalon Project at Yale Law School. www.yale.edu/lawweb/avalon/president/inaug/lincoln1.html.

59. Civics Online, http://www.civics-online.org/library/formatted/texts/jeff_davis.html.

60. Goodspeed, p. 205.

61. Washington County Marriage Records, Book B, p. 307.

62. Bishop, *Loyalty on the Frontier, or Sketches of Union Men of the Southwest* (St. Louis: R. P. Studley & Co., 1863), p. 90.

63. Lemke, *The Life and Letters of Judge David Walker*, pp. 101-102.

64. *Flashback* Vol. 37 #2, May 1987, pp. 32-33.

65. William Baxter, *Pea Ridge and Prairie Grove* (Cincinnati: Poe & Hitchcock, 1864), p. 8. Baxter will be quoted estensively through the first four chapters of this book. These will not be further footnoted as all quotations by him are from this book.

66. Kim A Scott, "The Legacy of Elias Moore," *Flashback*, Vol. 37, #4, Nov. 1987, pp. 28-29.

67. *Northwest Arkansas Times*, May 2, 1976.

68. Pat Carr, *In Fine Spirits: The Civil War Letters of Ras Stirman* (Fayetteville: Washington County Historical Society, 1986), pp. 18-19.

69. Lemke, *The Life and Letters of Judge David Walker*.

70. Carr, p. 18.

71. Carr, p. 19.

72. Lemke, *The Life and Letters of Judge David Walker*.

73. Goodspeed, Volume 2, p. 1002.

74. Fayetteville Public Library, Holcomb Family Papers.

75. Fayetteville Public Library, Van Hoose Family Papers.

76. Goodspeed, p. 232.

77. Kim Allen Scott, "Witness for the Prosecution: The Civil War Letters of Lieutenant George Taylor." *Arkansas Historical Quarterly,* Autumn 1989, pp 260-271.

78. Banes, p. 91.

79. Adeline Blakely Slave Narrative, p. 15.

80. Second Inaugural Address of Jefferson Davis, www.pointsouth.com/csanet/greatmen/davis/pres-ad2.htm

81. Banes, pp. 92-94.

82. U.S. War Department, *The War of the Rebelluion: A compilation of the Official Records of the Union and Confederate Armies*, 128 volumes (hereafter designated as *"O.R."*), Series 1, Volume 8, p. 69.

83. Goodspeed, p. 246.

84. O.R., Series I, Volume 8, p. 69.

85. Adeline Blakely Slave Narrative, p. 14.

86. Banes, p. 99-100.

87. Banes, p. 100.

88. Goodspeed, pp. 227-228.

89. Lemke, *The Life and Letters of Judge David Walker*, p. 93.

90. *Flashback*, Vol. 5 #5, October 1955, p. 31.

91. Albert W. Bishop, *An Oration Delivered at Fayetteville, Arkansas, July 4, 1865* (New York: 1865).

92. O.R., Series 3, Vol. 2, p. 958.

93. Goodspeed, p 227.

94. Banes, pp. 106-109.

95. Lemke, *The Life and Letters of Judge David Walker*.

96. Jay Monaghan, *Civil War on the Western Border 1854-1865* (Boston, Little, Brown & Company, 1955), pp. 261-262.

97. Adeline Blakely Slave Narrative, p. 185.

98. Furry, p. 7.

99. *Flashback*, Vol. 12 #4, Dec 1962.

100. Goodspeed, p. 229.

101. Ira Russell Papers (MC581), documents nos. 1 and 3, Special Collections, University of Arkansas Libraries, Fayetteville.

102. Robert W. Mecklin, numerous letters 1863 to 1864, Walter J. Lemke (MSL541). Series 10, Box 4. Special Collections, University of Arkansas Libraries, Fayetteville. Hereafter, all statements by Mecklin are from this source.

103. Furry, pp. 13-15.

104. Regiment Records, Union Regiments from Arkansas, First Regiment of Cavalry, under the name of Thomas J. Hunt, National Archives microfilm.

105. Lemke, *The Life and Letters of Judge David Walker*, pp. 60-65.

106. O.R., Series I, Vol. 22, part I, p. 312.

107. O.R., Series I, Vol. 22, part II, p. 191.

108. O.R., Series I, Vol. 22, part I, p. 306.

109. Sarah J. Yeater, "My Experiences During the War Between the States," *Arkansas Historical Quarterly*, Vol IV, No 1 (Spring 1945).

110. Elizur B. Harrison, "The Battle of Fayetteville," *Flashback*, May 1968, Vol. 18, #2, pp. 18-19.

111. Regimental Records Marcus LaRue Harrison.

112. O.R., Series I, Vol. 22, Part I, pp. 312-313.

113. Ibid., 306.

114. Regimental Records of Marcus LaRue Harrison.

115. O.R., Series I, Vol. 22, Part I, p. 311.

116. Edwin S. Walker, Ed., *Genealogical Notes of the Carpenter Family*, (Springfield, Illinois: No Publisher Stated, 1907), pp. 142-143.

117. Elizur B. Harrison, pp. 18-19.

118. O.R., Series I, Vol. 22, Part I, p. 312.

119. Yeater.

120. O.R., Series I, Vol. 22, Part I, p. 309.

121. O.R., Series I, Vol. 22, Part II, p. 829.

122. Bishop, p. 217.

123. O.R., Series I, Vol. 22, Part. I, p. 311.

124. O.R., Series I, Vol. 22, Part II, p. 246.

125. *Flashback*, Vol. 37 #4, Nov. 1987, p. 2.

126. History of the Fayetteville Post Office, January 1996, p. 2.

127. O.R. Series I, Vol 22, Part I, pp 594-595.

128. O.R., Series I, Vol. 22, Part I, pp. 594-595.

129. Mecklin papers.

130. Mecklin papers.

131. Adline Blakely Slave Narrative, p. 13.

132. Seabe Tuttle Slave Narrative. Slave Narratives from the Federal Writers' Project, 1936-1938. Arkansas Bnarratives, Volume II, Part 1. Interview of Seabe Tuttle by Zillah Cross Peel.

133. Lemke, *The Life and Letters of Judge David Walker*, p. 69.

134. P 27 The Life and Letters of Judge David Walker, compiled and edited by W.J. Lemke, Fayetteville 1957. WCHS

135. Mecklin papers.

136. Mecklin papers.

137. O.R., Series I, Vol,. 22, Part I, pp. 702-703.

138. Daniel E. Sutherland, Ed., *Guerrillas, Unionists, and Violence on the Confederate Home Front*, (Fayetteville: University of Arkansas Press, 1999), p. 175.

139. "Civil War Letters of Corporal David W. Badger," *Flashback*, Vol. 47 #1, Feb. 1997, p. 28.

140. First Arkansas Union Cavalry Regimental Records of Joseph S. Robb.

141. First Arkansas Union Cavalry Regiment Records of Marcus LaRue Harrison.

142. First Arkansas Union Cavalry Regiment Records of Jacob H. Keiser.

143. Sutherland, p. 181.

144. First Arkansas Union Cavalry Regiment Returns of Company M.

145. *Flashback*, Vol. 6, #4, July 1956, p. 5.

146. Lemke, Ed., *The Walker Family Letters*, no pagination.

147. Ibid.

148. Ibid

149. *Flashback* Vol. 6 #4, July 1956 pp 5-6.

150. Lemke, Judge David Walker, p 51.

151. Lemke, Ed., *The Walker Family Letters*, no pagination.

152. Oath of Mary Stone, June 20, 1864. Sue Walker Papers (MC 11), series 4, box 1, folder 4. Special Collections, University of Arkansas Libraries, Fayetteville.

153. Bishop, Loyalty on the Frontier.

154. First Arkansas Union Cavalry Regiment Records of Thomas Wilhite.

155. First Arkansas Union Cavalry Regiment Records of Jesse Gilstrap.

156. O.R., Series I, Vol, 22, Part II, p. 149.

157. O.R., Series I, Vol. 41, Party I, pp. 397-398.

158. *Flashback*, Vol. 5, #5, Oct. 1955, p. 31.

159. Lemke, *Judge David Walker*, p. 103.

160. Letter from Mrs. J. L. Matlock, Walker book p 105

161. Lemke, *Judge David Walker*, pp. 52.

162. Lemke, *Judge David Walker*, p. 53.

Index

Alexander, William 106

Arrington, Alfed 22

Arrington, Alfred Jr. 22, 89

Arrington, Annette 22

Arrington, Sarah 22, 89

Asboth, Alexander 64-67

Bams, James 25

Barber, Cyrus 98

Barker, Edward - 110-111

Barnes, James 16

Barringtonm, Elizabeth 21

Battenfield, Jacob 16, 112

Baxter, Fidelia 25

Baxter, William 5, 9, 10, 25, 44, 49, 52, 60-72, 74, 77-79, 82, 83, 90, 98, 111, 126, 131

Bean, Mark 26

Beauford Stephen 15

Bedford, Stephen 30, 38

Bell, Jim 98

Bell, John 25-28, 31-36

Bell, Samuel 17, 43, 47, 49, 51, 54, 112

Bennett, Lyman 110

Billingsley, John 39, 40

Bills, Absalom 14

Bingham, Thomas 98

Binner, Samuel 16

Bishop, Albert W. 75, 96, 100, 101, 103, 108

Bishop, Outsen 14

Blake, Robert 15

Blakely, Adeline 28-30, 62, 68, 79, 87, 111

Blakely, Albert 15

Blakely, Elizabeth 15, 62, 79, 110

Blakely, John 15, 28

Blakely, Leonora 15

Blunt, James G. 78, 114

Boals, Robert 16

Bonhome, Richard 14

Boone, Benjamin F. 30, 34, 37, 38, 44, 48, 56, 73, 81, 82

Boone, Cener 44

Boone, Ewlar 30

Boone, James 29-30-34

Boone, Lafayette 21, 30, 44, 51, 52

Boswell, Hugh 15

Botefuhr, Hugo 96, 128

Boudinot, Elias 4, 11, 30, 43, 51, 57

Bowen, John 130

Bowers, William 14

Bramon, A. 13

Bramon, Olivia 13

Brandenburg, John 15, 25, 51, 56, 73

Breckenridge, John C. 31-36

Brooks, William H. 48, 56, 73, 77, 81, 114, 123, 129

Brown, Egbert 75

Brown, William (Buck) 110, 128, 129, 132

Buchanan, Robert 43

Buckner, Simon B. 134

Buie, John 11, 15, 89

Butterfield, Charles 2, 4, 14, 30, 33, 53

Butterfield, John 3

Butterfield, Mary - 14

Byrnside, Margaret 3, 8, 25

Cabell, William L. 91-110

Caffee, Amos 103

Calfry, Henry 16

Calfry, Randolph 15, 73

Calfry, William 16

Campbell, Matilda 128

Cannon, Francis W. 98

Carlile, James 16, 89

Carlile, Joshua 16

Carnahan, Mr. 121

Carpenter, Seymour D. 103, 104, 106, 108, 109

Casey, Elizabeth 16, 22

Cate, John 5, 16

Cato, John 14

Chapman, Benjamin 13

Chapman, Margaret 14

Choran, Amos 16

Churchwell, James 14

Clark, George 16

Clark, Mary 8

Clemmons, Nick 27

Cleveland, Ira 15

Coffee, Maurice 14

Cooper, Elmore 16

Corwin, Cornelia 10

Cox, John 34

Crawford, John 21, 34, 52

Crouch, Addison 4, 16, 30

Cunningham, Leroy 21

Cunningham, William 24

Curtis, Samuel R. 65, 107, 109, 118, 120, 127

Daniels, Mary 8

Darneal, James 4

Darter, Alexander 15

Davenport, Charles 90

Davenport, Malvinia 90

Davidson, Elijah 15, 56

Davidson, Matthew 56

Davidson, Perry 56

Davidson, Sallie 8

Davis, Jefferson 39, 42, 43, 59, 63, 64, 90, 91, 134

Dawson, Edward 15

Dean, Charles 32, 38, 39, 40, 43, 45, 55

Dean, Perry 34

Denton, Louis 14

Dick, David 14

Dickson, Joseph 15, 16, 20, 45, 62

Dickson, Sarah 45

Diester, Alexander 15

Dorsey, Caleb 97, 100

Doss, J.P. 43

Douglas, Stephen A. 31-36

Duke, M.C. 38, 48, 73, 81

Dunlap, Jefferson 15, 73

Dunom, Solomon 15

Elliott, William 14, 73

Fagan, James F. 128, 129

Fahagen, Squire 27

Feemster, Annie 8

Feemster, Jane 8

Feemster, Martha 110

Feemster, Mercus 10, 110

Fishburn Eli 14

Fishburn, Sara 14

Fisher, Albert 14

Fitch, Ezra 96, 100, 103, 104

Flanagin, Harris 112

Fletcher, John 15

Ford, Henry 16

Foster, Lucretia - see Smith, Lucretia

Fox, Roger 15, 89

Frazer, John 15, 52, 56

Frazer, Martin 15

Freyschlag, Mr. 121

Fuver, Henry 14

Gaines, Benjamin 13, 27

Gaines, Sally 13

Gannett, Richard 16

Gartman, Richard 14, 89

Gilstrap, Jesse 125-127

Gilstrap, Thomas 24, 75

Glass, Hugh 15, 73

Graham, Littleton 13

Graham, Mariah 76

Graham, Robert 2, 8, 9, 11, 23, 76

Gregg, Lafayette 11, 20, 34, 115, 122, 124

Gregg, Mary 20, 122

Gunter, Jennie 121

Gunter, Thomas 4, 20, 39, 40, 45, 52, 57, 73, 76

Hackett, Nelson 12, 29

Ham, Elijah 98

Hannah, Richard 10

Harrell, John M. 97

Harrell, Robert 16

Harrison, Elizur B. 95-104, 128

Harrison, Marcus LaRue 75, 88, 90-110, 114-118, 123, 128, 129

Hart, Columbus 73

Hauptman, Charles 15, 115

Hawkins, Jane 27, 48, 54, 55

Hawkins, Martin 21, 48, 54, 55

Heath, Martha 22

Henry, Catherine 120

Henry, Isaac 120-121

Henry, Lucy 14

Henry, Marshall 48, 54, 122

Henry, Martha 16, 17, 22

Henry, William 16

Henlsey, James 73, 74

Herron, Francis 78, 79, 89, 107

Hindman, Thomas J. 57, 72, 77, 78, 80-82

Hines, Thomas 16

Hodges, Robert 73

Hogan, Robert 15

Holcomb, Joseph 15, 30, 34, 44, 57

Holderness, Algemanus 106

Hopkins, DeWitt 98, 128

Houghs, Charles 13

Houghs, Melinda 13

House, George 14

House, Warren 14

Howland, Mary 10

Hughey, William M. 97-100

Hunt, Thomas J. 24, 76, 89, 90, 96, 114, 115, 127, 128

Hutchinson, James 103

Inger, Susan 27

Jackson, Columbus 16

Jackson, James 16

Jobe, Daniel 14, 89

Johnson, James M. 89

Johnson, John K. 120

Jones, Daniel 16

Jordan, Bradburn 16

Keiser, Jacob 118

Keller, John 13

Keller, Mary 13

Kelly, Thomas 51

Kice, R.B. 17

Lancaster, Leroy 15

Lee, Robert E. 110, 133, 134

Leeper, Matthew 13, 21, 23, 36

Lewis, Augustus 51

Lewis, John 15

Lewis, Joseph 13, 51, 111

Lewis, Mary 51

Lincoln, Abraham 31-36, 40-42, 45, 87, 129-133

Love, Ganet 14

Luper, Gilbert 98

Mack, Rowen E.M. 96

Macy, James 15

McClellan, George 129-130

McCollum, Albert 56

McCulloch, Benjamin 55, 59, 61, 66, 68, 69, 71, 76. 77

McCulloch, Clem 76, 81

McGarrah, Andrew 51

McGarrah, Elizabeth (mother) 6, 89

McGarrah, Elizabeth (daughter) 6

McGarrah, James 7

McGarrah, Matthew 73, 89

McGarrah, Sarah 7

McGarrah, William 6, 13, 89

McIlroy, H.J. 73

McIlroy, William 15

McIntosh, James 69, 71

McNeil, John 115, 127

McRoy, Henry 14, 89

McRoy, Julia 14

McRoy, Jack 38, 48

Mecklin, Robert 8, 9, 32, 85, 111-113, 118

Messenger, William 98

Miller, Elizabeth 21

Miller, George 21

Miller, Martha 13, 21

Miller, William 13, 21

Monroe, James C. 100, 101, 103, 106, 108

Moore, Elias 12, 44, 48, 49, 54

Moore, James 16, 52, 73

Moore, William 12, 16, 77

Morrow, John 16

Mullis, Mr. 30

Murphy, Isaac 46

Musser 118

Neal, W.T. 39, 40

Nolen, Mrs. 111

North, George 24

Onstott, John 4

Ormsby, Waterman L. 2, 3, 5

Orr, John 97

Osburne, Jonathan 15

Outzen, Ausmus 15

Paddock, Frank 18

Paddock, Mary 18

Palmer, John R. 17, 48, 74, 109

Parks, J.H. 4, 6

Parks, James 56, 100

Parks, John O. 73

Parks, John P.A. 28, 29, 39, 40, 52, 111

Parris, James 14

Peer, Amanda 11, 13

Peer, Edward 15

Peer, Jacob 13

Peer, John 15

Peerson, W.C. 74, 130

Pegram, Benjamin 13, 121

Pegram, Mary 13

Perkins, James 17

Perkins, John 16, 73

Pettigrew, James R. 4, 11, 19, 24, 30, 45, 51, 73, 81, 123

Pettigrew, Sarah 19

Pettigrew, Willis 27

Pettigrew, Zeb 32, 34

Phelps, John 75

Phillips, William A. 92

Pike, Albert 47, 56

Pollard, Ann 17

Pollard, James 52, 73, 81, 82

Pollard, John 48, 52, 56

Pollard, Mary 17, 50, 51

Pollard, Thomas Jefferson 11, 17, 32, 38, 56, 70, 112

Pollard, Thomas Jefferson Jr. 15, 17, 48, 50, 54, 56

Pollard, Wade 17, 30, 112
Pope, Margaret 22, 27
Price, Sterling 60, 68, 128, 131
Pratt, Edward 16
Purdy, Mr. 121
Pyeatt, James 16
Quarles Martha 27
Quarles, Amry 27
Quarles, William 25, 27
Quarles, William 15, 23, 57
Quesenberry, William 11, 12, 32, 33, 56, 95, 123
Ramsey, John 16
Reagan, Alvira 45
Reagan, Wilburn 11, 19, 28, 32, 45, 66, 74
Rector, Henry 46
Reed, George 24, 75
Richardson, Charlie 27
Ridge, John 7
Ridge, Sara 7
Rieff, Americus 51, 55, 74
Rieff, Henry 15, 24
Rieff, Joseph 15
Riley, George 15
Robb, Joseph S. 94, 100, 103, 104, 115, 116
Rollins, Thomas 16
Rosecrans, William 127
Roseman, James 119, 120
Russell, George 94

Russell, Ira 85
Russell, J.B. 38
Ruth, John 16, 112
Sawyer, Sophia 6, 7, 8
Scarborough, J.G. 17, 112
Schofield, James M. 77, 126
Scott, John 97
Searle, Elhannon 96, 98, 101
Shipley, Ann 14
Shipley, Henry 14
Simon, Tracy 4
Simpson, J.B. 4
Smith, E. Kirby 134
Smith, Felen 14
Smith, George 16
Smith, Jackson 8
Smith, James 16, 56
Smith, John 56
Smith, Lucretia 8, 47
Smith, Mary 122
Smith, Presley 21, 34, 55, 68, 122
Smith, Randall 101
Smith, William 16, 48, 56
Smithson, Cynthia 21
Smithson, David 17, 34, 112
Smithson, Samuel 73
Smithson, William 24, 25, 114
Springer, Francis 5, 80, 84, 88
Stafford, Amos 15
Stanford, Steele 56

Stanton, Edwin M. 132

Steele, William 91, 107

Stevenson, James 17, 18, 112, 121

Stigowest, Edward 15

Striman, Erastus (Ras) 48, 53, 55, 71

Stirman, James H. 4, 8, 11, 15, 16, 23, 38, 39, 40

Stirman, James W. 48

Stirman, Rebecca 17, 53

Stone, Dave 33

Stone, Jim 33

Stone, Mary 47, 124, 125

Stone, Stephen K. 15, 38, 125

Strickland, Mary 22

Sutton, Isabella 21

Sutton, Henry 21

Sutton, James 15, 16, 21, 74

Sutton, Seneca 21

Taylor, George 17, 38, 60, 112

Taylor, Isaac 3, 26, 51, 73

Taylor, Whitson 15

Tebbetts, Jonas 10, 14, 18, 20, 23, 25, 46, 47, 53, 62-64, 66, 74, 76

Tebbetts, Marian 1, 10, 18, 23, 24, 25, 27, 28, 30, 62, 63, 64, 68, 70, 76

Tebbetts, Matilda 17, 18, 20, 25, 28

Tefft, Jonathan 101

Thomas, Hugh 32

Thomas, John 15

Thompson, Lee L. 97, 100

Tifanaur, Clinton 15

Tuttle, James 24

Tuttle, Seabe 111, 112

Uncary, Thomas 17, 112

Van Dorn, Earl 67

Van Dyke, Henry 16

Vaney, William 21

Van Hoose, Bud 57

Van Hoose, Elizabeth 47

Van Hoose, George 57, 132, 133

Van Hoose, James 8, 12, 15, 24, 30, 32, 38, 132, 133

Van Hoose, Martha 117

Van Hoose, Melinda 132

Van Hoose, Peter 4, 21, 23, 24, 34

Van Horne, Thomas 10, 11, 53

Van Winkle, Sam 27

Vertal, Jane 13

Vertal, Jerry 13

Voorhees, James 16

Walker, David 7, 14, 18, 23, 32, 33, 36-40, 43, 46, 54, 55, 57, 74, 77. 90, 91, 112, 121, 122, 131, 133

Walker, David Jr. 122

Walker, James David 18, 19, 32, 43, 52, 76, 121

Walker, Jane 7, 19

Walker, Mary 18, 19, 54, 55, 76

Walker, Vol 18

Walker, Whiting 81

Walker, Wythe 4, 24, 30, 52, 123

Wallace, Alfred 29
Ward, S.M. 15, 73
Washburn, Josiah 12
Washington, Rebecca 22, 23
Washington, Whiting 13, 22, 23
Watson, Christiana 48
Watson, Clara 11
Watson, Frank 15, 48, 73
Watson, William 15, 34, 44
Wax, Nicholas 48, 54
Wells, Crittenden C. 90, 98
Wheeler, Emily Walker 37
White, Ebeneezer 16
White, William 15
Whitmore, James 16
Wilhite, Thomas 45, 125, 126
Williams, Isaac 15
Williford, Henry 15, 51, 56, 73, 82, 89
Williford, Martha 51
Williford, Nelson 15, 51, 56, 73, 81, 82, 89
Williford, Seneca 15, 89
Williford, Thomas 15, 51
Wilson, Alfred M. 19, 31, 32, 34, 38, 55, 721, 74, 121
Wilson, Isabella 19
Wilson, James K. 73
Wilson, John 21, 73, 123
Wilson, Kate 25
Wilson, Washington 15, 23, 25, 29, 118

Woods, Forrest 15
Woods, John 15
Woods, Richard 15
Worthington, John 132
Yeater, Sara 95, 97, 106
Yell, Archibald 19
Zellieh, Charlotta 5
Zellieh, Joseph 5, 16
Zellner, Ferdinand 10, 68

www.ingramcontent.com/pod-product-compliance
Lightning Source LLC
Chambersburg PA
CBHW061656040426
42446CB00010B/1763